PLATONISM IN ENGLISH POETRY

OF THE SIXTEENTH AND
SEVENTEENTH CENTURIES

PLATONISM IN ENGLISH POETRY

OF THE SIXTEENTH AND SEVENTEENTH CENTURIES

BY

JOHN SMITH HARRISON

NEW YORK

RUSSELL & RUSSELL · INC

1965

Columbia University

STUDIES IN COMPARATIVE LITERATURE

FIRST PUBLISHED IN 1903

REISSUED, 1965, BY RUSSELL & RUSSELL, INC.

BY ARRANGEMENT WITH JOHN SMITH HARRISON

L. C. CATALOG CARD NO: 65-17898

PRINTED IN THE UNITED STATES OF AMERICA

TO

My Father and My Mother

PREFACE

THIS essay was presented as a dissertation for the doctorate in Columbia University. It attempts to explain the nature of the influence of Platonism upon English poetry of the sixteenth and seventeenth centuries, exclusive of the drama. Its method is purely critical. It has not attempted to treat the subject from the standpoint of the individual poet, but has tried to interpret the whole body of English poetry of the period under survey as an integral output of the spiritual thought and life of the time.

In its interpretation of this body of poetry the essay has aimed to see Platonism in its true historical perspective, as it must have been understood by the poets, either as a system of philosophic thought held consciously in the mind, or as a more intimate possession of the spirit in its outlook upon life. The idea of Platonism which these poets had was that which Ficino had made known to Italy of the

fifteenth century, and from Italy to the rest of
Europe. Ficino saw Plato through two more
or less refracting media. To him Plato was
the "divine Plato," the importance of whose
work lay in its subtle affinity for the forms
of Christian thought. He thus Christianized
Plato's philosophy. But this body of thought
was that peculiar product resulting from the
study of Plato's "Dialogues" in the light of
what latter-day criticism has named Neo-platonism, or that new form of Platonic philosophy
which is expounded in the "Enneads" of Plotinus. But more than this. Ficino endeavored
to reform the practice of love by the application of the Platonic doctrine of love and beauty
to the lover's passion. From his "Commentarium in Convivium," which he translated into
Italian, originate the various discussions of love
and beauty from the Platonic standpoint which
were carried on in dialogues and manuals of
court etiquette throughout the sixteenth century. In this essay, consequently, reference
has been made to Ficino's "Commentarium"
on the points involved in the theory of love
and beauty. The translations have been made
directly from the Latin version of the commentary. On the more metaphysical side of
Platonism the "Enneads" of Plotinus have

been accepted as representative. The translation on page 77 is taken from Mr. Bigg's "Neo-
Platonism," and those on pages 153, 154, 155
are from Thomas Taylor's translation noted
in the bibliography. In interpreting the "Enneads" I have accepted the explanation of his
system by Mr. Whittaker in "The Neo-Platonists." All the quotations from Plato's "Dialogues" are from Jowett's translation. In
quoting from the poets the texts of the editions
noted in the bibliography have been followed
in details of spelling, punctuation, and the
like.

In the preparation of the work hardly anything of a critical nature was found serviceable.
In the notes to the works of the individual
poets several detached references are to be
gratefully mentioned, but no general appreciation of the part Platonism played in the work
of the English poets was at hand. Mr. Fletcher's article on the "Précieuses at the Court of
Charles I," in the second number of the "Journal of Comparative Literature," appeared after
this essay had gone to the printer.

I should like to acknowledge my thanks to
Mr. W. H. Heck for his service of transcrip-
tion in the British Museum Library and to
Miss M. P. Conant for a similar kindness in
research work in the Harvard College Library.

To Professor George Edward Woodberry I am most deeply grateful for innumerable suggestions and invaluable advice. The work was undertaken at his suggestion, and throughout the past two years has progressed under his kindly criticism. But the help and inspiration which I have received from him antedate the inception of the essay, extending back to the earlier days of undergraduate life. The work is thus inseparably connected with the training in the study of literature which he has given, and his help in its completion is only an episode in a long series of kindnesses which he has been ever willing to show.

ORANGE, N.J.,
June 1, 1903.

CONTENTS

CHAPTER I

CHAPTER II

CHAPTER III

PLATONISM IN ENGLISH POETRY

CHAPTER I

IDEALS OF CHRISTIAN VIRTUES

I. HOLINESS

THE fundamental doctrine of Platonism as it was understood throughout the period of the sixteenth and seventeenth centuries was the reality of a heavenly beauty known in and by the soul, as contrasted with an earthly beauty known only to the sense. In this the Christian philosophic mind found the basis for its conception of holiness. Christian discipline and Platonic idealism blended in the " Faerie Queene " in the legend of the Red Cross Knight.

The underlying idea taught by Spenser in the first book is that holiness is a state of the soul in which wisdom or truth can be seen and loved in and for its beauty. In the allegorical scheme of his work Una stands for the Platonic

1

wisdom, σοφία, or ἀρετή, and a sight of her in
her native beauty constitutes the happy ending
of the many struggles and perplexities that the
Red Cross Knight experiences in his pursuit of
holiness. The identification of Una with the
Platonic idea of truth or wisdom is not merely
a matter of inference left for the reader to
draw ; for Spenser himself is careful to inform
us of the true nature of the part she plays in
his allegory. Una is presented as teaching the
satyrs truth and " trew sacred lore." (I. vi. 19 ;
I. vi. 30.) When the lion, amazed at her sight,
forgets his fierceness, Spenser comments :

> " O how can beautie maister the most strong,
> And simple truth subdue avenging wrong?"
>
> (I. iii. 6.)

When Una summons Arthur to the rescue of
the Red Cross Knight from the Giant and the
Dragon, Spenser opens his canto with a reflection on the guiding power of grace and truth
amid the many perils of human life :

> " Ay me, how many perils doe enfold
> The righteous man, to make him daily fall?
> Were not, that heavenly grace doth him uphold,
> And stedfast truth acquite him out of all.
> Her love is firme, her care continuall,

> So oft as he through his owne foolish pride,
> Or weaknesse is to sinfull bands made thrall."
>
> (I. viii. 1.)

Here Arthur is meant by grace and Una by truth. In accordance with the same conception of Una's nature Satyrane is made to wonder

> "at her wisedome heavenly rare,
> Whose like in womens wit he never knew;
>
> *   *   *   *   *
>
> Thenceforth he kept her goodly company,
> And learnd her discipline of faith and veritie."
>
> (I. vi. 31.)

Furthermore, she is represented as guiding the Red Cross Knight to Fidelia's school, where he is to taste her "heavenly learning," to hear the wisdom of her divine words, and to learn "celestiall discipline." (I. x. 18.) In making these comments and in thus directing the course of the action of his poem Spenser presents in Una the personification of truth or wisdom.

But he does more than this ; he presents her not only as wisdom, but as true beauty. Spenser is so thoroughly convinced of the truth of that fundamental idea of Platonic ethics, that truth and beauty are identical, that he shows their union in the character of Una,

in whom, as her name signifies, they are one.
Plato had taught that the highest beauty
which the soul can know is wisdom, which,
though invisible to sight, would inflame the
hearts of men in an unwonted degree could
there be a visible image of her.   In his
"Phædrus" he had stated that "sight is the
most piercing of our bodily senses; though not
by that is wisdom seen; her loveliness would
have been transporting if there had been a
visible image of her."   (250.)   Convinced, as
Spenser was, of the spiritual nature of the
beauty of wisdom, he carefully avoids dwelling upon any detail of Una's physical beauty.
The poetic form of allegory, through which his
ideas were to be conveyed, required the personification of truth, and the romantic character of
chivalry demanded that his Knight should have
a lady to protect.   The progress of the action
of the poem, moreover, made necessary some
reference to the details of Una's form and feature.   (Cf. I. iii. 4–6; vi. 9.)   But in no instance where the physical form of Una is
brought to notice is there any trace of the
poet's desire to concentrate attention upon
her physical charms.   In this respect Una

stands distinctly apart from all his other heroines, and especially Belphœbe. And yet Spenser has taken the greatest care to show that the source of Una's influence over those that come into her presence lies in the power exerted by her beauty ; but this is the beauty of her whole nature, a penetrating radiance of light revealing the soul that is truly wise. Indeed, when Spenser has the best of opportunities to describe Una, after she has laid aside the black stole that hides her features, he contents himself with a few lines, testifying only to their radiant brilliancy :

> " Her angels face
> As the great eye of heaven shyned bright,
> And made a sunshine in the shadie place."
> (I. iii. 4.)

In other instances he directs our attention to the power which the mere sight of her has upon the beholder. Her beauty can tame the raging lion and turn a ravenous beast into a strong body-guard who finds his duty in the light of her fair eyes :

> " It fortuned out of the thickest wood
> A ramping Lyon rushed suddainly,
> Hunting full greedie after salvage blood ;

Soone as the royall virgin he did spy,
With gaping mouth at her ran greedily,
To have attonce devour'd her tender corse:
But to the pray when as he drew more ny,
His bloudie rage asswaged with remorse,
And with the sight amazd, forgat his furious forse."

(I. iii. 5.)

"The Lyon would not leave her desolate,

*   *   *   *   *

From her faire eyes he tooke commaundement,
And ever by her lookes conceived her intent."

(I. iii. 9.)

The wild-wood gods stand astonished at her
beauty, and in their wonder pity her desolate
condition. (I. vi. 9–12.) Old Sylvanus is
smitten by a sight of her. In her presence he
doubts the purity of his own Dryope's fairness; sometimes he thinks her Venus, but then
on further reflection he recalls that Venus
never had so sober mood; her image calls to
mind —

"His ancient love, and dearest *Cyparisse*,

*   *   *   *   *

How fair he was, and yet not faire to this."

(I. vi. 17.)

To behold her lovely face the wood nymphs
flock about and when they have seen it, they
flee away in envious fear, lest the contrast of

its beauty may disgrace their own. (I. vi. 18.) By these dramatic touches Spenser very skilfully suggests to his reader the high nature of Una's beauty. It has a power to win its way upon the brute creation, and it has a severity and radiance that set it off from the beauty of physical form possessed by the wood nymphs and even by the great goddess of love, Venus.

The most important consideration that bears upon the question of Una's beauty is found in the method which Spenser has used to indicate how the Red Cross Knight attains to a knowledge of it. One reason why the people of the wood, the nymphs, the fauns, and the satyrs, were permitted to see the celestial beauty of Una unveiled lay in the fact that through their experiences a means was provided by the poet to quicken the imagination into a sense of its pure nature. But the Knight, though he had journeyed with her throughout a great portion of her " wearie journey," had never been able to see her face in its native splendor, hidden, as it had always been, from his sight by the black veil which Una wore. The deep conceit which Spenser here uses points in the direction of Platonism ; for there it

was taught that wisdom could be seen only
by the soul. This is a fundamental truth,
present everywhere in Plato, in the vision of
beauty that rises before the mind at the end
of the dialectic of the "Symposium," in the
species of divine fury that accompanies the
recollection of the ideal world in the presence
of a beautiful object, as analyzed in the
"Phædrus," and in the "Hymn of the Dialectic" in the "Republic" by which the soul
rises to a sight of the good. (VII. 532.) In
the "Phædo" the function of philosophy is
explained to lie in the exercise by the soul of
this power of spiritual contemplation of true
existence. (82, 83.) In Spenser this conception is further illustrated by the part which
the schooling, received by the Red Cross Knight
on the Mount of Contemplation, played in the
perfection of his mental vision. Up to the
time when the Knight comes to the Mount
he is, as the aged sire says, a "man of earth,"
and his spirit needs to be purified of all the
grossness of sense. (I. x. 52.) When this has
been accomplished, the Knight is prepared to

> " see the way,
> That never yet was seene of Faeries sonne."
>
> (I. x. 52.)

While on this Mount he is initiated into a knowledge of the glories of the Heavenly Jerusalem, and through this experience he is made aware of the relative insignificance of that beauty which he had thought the greatest to be known on earth. He thus says to the aged man, Heavenly Contemplation, who has revealed this vision to him :

" Till now, said then the knight, I weened well,
   That great *Cleopolis*, where I have beene,
   In which that fairest *Faerie Queene* doth dwell,
   The fairest Citie was, that might be seene ;
   And that bright towre all built of christall cleene,
   Panthea, seemd the brightest thing, that was :
   But now by proofe all otherwise I weene ;
   For this great Citie that does far surpas,
   And this bright Angels towre quite dims that towre of
      glas."   (I. x. 58.)

With his soul filled with the radiance of this vision of beauty, his eyes dazed —

" Through passing brightnesse, which did quite confound
   His feeble sence, and too exceeding shyne.
   So darke are earthly things compard to things divine — "
                                            (I. x. 67.)

the Red Cross Knight descends from the Mount; and when after the completion of his labors he sees Una on the day of her betrothal, he wonders at a beauty in her which he has never before seen. Una has now laid aside her black veil, and shines upon him in the native undimmed splendor of truth.

" The blazing brightnesse of her beauties beame,
  And glorious light of her sunshyny face
  To tell, were as to strive against the streame.
  My ragged rimes are all too rude and bace,
  Her heavenly lineaments for to enchace.
  Ne wonder; for her owne deare loved knight,
  All were she dayly with himselfe in place,
  Did wonder much at her celestiall sight:
  Oft had he seene her faire, but never so faire dight."

(I. xii. 23.)

The contribution of Platonism to the formation of the ideal of holiness can now be easily recognized. The discipline of the Red Cross Knight in the House of Holiness is twofold. In the practice of the Christian graces — faith, hope, and charity — the Knight is perfected in the way of the righteous life. He is a penitent seeking to cleanse his soul of the infection of sin. On the Mount of Heavenly Contemplation he exercises his soul in the contemplative vision of the eternal world. But the emphasis laid by Platonism upon the loveliness of that wisdom which is the object of contemplation results in quickening the imagination

and in stirring the soul to realize the principle
in love. This is the exact nature of the experience of the Red Cross Knight at the end
of his journey. On the Mount of Heavenly
Contemplation he has a desire to remain in the
peaceful contemplation of heaven :

> " O let me not (quoth he) then turne againe
> Backe to the world, whose joyes so fruitlesse are ;
> But let me here for aye in peace remaine,
> Or streight way on that last long voyage fare,
> That nothing may my present hope empare."
>
> (I. x. 63.)

But the aged sire, Heavenly Contemplation,
reminds him of his duty to free Una's parents
from the dragon. (I. x. 63.) Obedient but still
purposing to return to the contemplative life
(I. x. 64), the Knight descends ; and in the
performance of his duty he gains the reward
that the contemplative life brings. " But he,"
says Plato, " whose initiation is recent, and who
has been the spectator of many glories in the
other world, is amazed when he sees any one having a godlike face or any bodily form which is
the expression of divine beauty." (" Phædrus,"
251.) Thus it is that the Red Cross Knight

> " Did wonder much at her celestiall sight."
>
> (I. xii. 23.)

With that sight comes the one joy of his life after the many struggles experienced in the perfection of his soul in holiness.

" And ever, when his eye did her behold,
His heart did seeme to melt in pleasures manifold."

(I. xii. 40.)

II. TEMPERANCE

The spiritual welfare of the soul was the prime object of importance to the Christian. Through the power of its doctrine of heavenly beauty Platonism had entered into the conception of this life considered in its heavenward aspect. It remained to show how it could explain the right manner of conduct for the soul in the presence of those strong passions which were felt as the disturbing elements of its inner welfare. In the Platonic system of morality there was a conception of temperance, σωφροσύνη, based upon an analysis of the soul sufficiently comprehensive to cover the entire scope of its activities; in fact, temperance was there conceived as the necessary condition for the presence of any virtue in the soul. The vitality of this teaching in English poetry is found in the second book of Spenser's

" Faerie Queene," celebrating the exploits of
the knight Guyon,

"In whom great rule of Temp'raunce goodly doth appeare."
(Introd., stz. 5.)

The adventures of Guyon, through the discipline of which he perfects himself in temperance, fall into two distinct groups. Up to the
sixth book the conflicts in which he is concerned
are those calculated to try his mastery of the
angry impulses of his nature. After the sixth
book his struggles record his proficiency in
governing the sensual desires of appetite. This
division is made in accordance with the analysis
of the soul on which Plato bases his doctrine of
temperance. Within the soul are three distinct
principles, — one rational and two irrational.
The irrational principles are, first, the irascible
impulse of spirit ($\theta\upsilon\mu\acute{o}\varsigma$) with which a man is
angry and, second, the appetitive instinct the
workings of which are manifested in all the sensual gratifications of the body, and in the love
of wealth. The rational principle is that of
reason by which a man learns truth. (" Republic," IX. 580, 581.) Against this one rational
principle the two irrational impulses are constantly insurgent, and temperance is that har-

mony or order resulting in the soul when the rational principle rules and the two irrational principles are obedient to its sovereignty. "And would you not say," asks Socrates, "that he is temperate who has these same elements in friendly harmony, in whom the one ruling principle of reason, and the two subject ones of spirit and desire are equally agreed that reason ought to rule, and do not rebel?" ("Republic," IV. 442.)

The rule of right reason in Guyon over his angry impulses is recorded in three instances; in each case the anger is aroused under varying conditions. The opening episode of the book presents Guyon checking the impetuous fury of his wrath when he learns that it has been aroused by a false presentation of the facts. Archimago, the deceitful enemy of truth, related to Guyon how the Red Cross Knight had violated the purity of a maiden ; and the pretended maiden herself became a party to the lie. (II. i. 10, 11, 17.) When Guyon heard of this outrage he hastened to avenge the wrong.

> " He staid not lenger talke, but with fierce ire
>   And zealous hast away is quickly gone
>   To seeke that knight."   (II. i. 13.)

And yet he wondered how the Red Cross
Knight could have done such a deed.   He
knew that he was a knight of honor and had
won glory in his defence of Una.   (II. i. 19.)
He was quick, then, to restrain himself when
about to charge upon the accused Knight, for
on his shield he recognized the cross of his
Lord.   When he was on the point of clashing
with his enemy, he

> " gan abace
> His threatned speare, as if some new mishap
> Had him betidde, or hidden daunger did entrap."
> (II. i. 26.)

After an apology and an exchange of knightly
courtesies with the Red Cross Knight he was
able to

> " turne his earnest unto game,
> Through goodly handing and wise temperance."
> (II. i. 31.)

The second encounter of Guyon with the
forces of wrath is the struggle with Furor and
his mother Occasion.   (II. iv. 3–36.)   He has
now to try his strength in conquering wrath
when it has an occasion to be aroused.   The
power with which he strives is described as
a fury of great might, but so ill-governed by

reason that in its blind passion its force is
spent to no purpose.

> " And sure he was a man of mickle might,
>   Had he had gouvernance, it well to guide :
>   But when the franticke fit inflamd his spright,
>   His force was vaine, and strooke more often wide,
>   Then at the aymed marke which he had eide :
>   And oft himselfe he chaunst to hurt unwares,
>   Whilst reason blent through passion, nought describe,
>   But as a blindfold Bull at randon fares,
>   And where he hits, nought knowes, and whom he hurts
>   nought cares."   (II. iv. 7.)

Guyon struggles with this madman and
finally, after he has quieted the reviling tongue
of Occasion, who urges her son, Furor, on to
the conflict, he binds him with iron chains.

> " In his strong armes he stiffely him embraste,
>   Who him gainstriving, nought at all prevaild :
>   For all his power was utterly defaste,
>   And furious fits at earst quite weren quaild :
>   Oft he re'nforst, and oft his forces fayld,
>   Yet yield he would not, nor his rancour slacke.
>   Then him to ground he cast, and rudely hayld,
>   And both his hands fast bound behind his backe,
>   And both his feet in fetters to an yron racke."
>   (II. iv. 14.)

The third trial of Guyon's reason is by a
species of wrath so wilfully furious that it

runs to seek an occasion for a quarrel, and finds no rest until it has succeeded. This type of irascible impulse is portrayed in Pyrochles. He delights in deeds of daring might, and in blood and spoil. (II. iv. 42.) His squire, Atin by name, acts as his forerunner to seek an occasion for his lord's furious delight. (II. iv. 43.) But Guyon masters himself both in his refusal to fight for no good reason, and in his behavior when forced against his wishes to a conflict with Pyrochles. Guyon bids Atin tell his master that he, Guyon, has bound Occasion, and the Palmer, who is the rational element of Guyon personified, lectures the squire on the folly of wilful anger.

> " Madman (said then the Palmer) that does seeke
> *Occasion* to wrath, and cause of strife;
> She comes unsought, and shonned followes eke.
> Happy, who can abstaine, when Rancour rife
> Kindles Revenge, and threats his rusty knife;
> Woe never wants, where every cause is caught,
> And rash *Occasion* makes unquiet life."
>
> (II. iv. 44.)

Even when Guyon is compelled by Pyrochles to the fight, the Knight does not give way to unrestrained wrath, but ever tempers his pas-

sion with reason.   In the conflict Pyrochles
thundered blows:

> " But *Guyon*, in the heat of all his strife,
> Was warie wise, and closely did awayt
> Avauntage, whilest his foe did rage most rife."
>
> (II. v. 9.)

When at last Guyon has his foe at his feet, he
spares his life, so firmly he holds his passion in
check.

> " Eftsoones his cruell hand Sir *Guyon* stayd,
> Tempring the passion with advisement slow,
> And maistring might on enimy dismayd."
>
> (II. v. 13.)

Thus far Guyon's life has exemplified the
rule of reason over the irrational element of
wrath; the remaining episodes of his life centre
about the struggle of the irrational element of
appetite.   In this his soul is tried in three
various forms of sensual desire.   In Phædria
the first form is typified.   She represents the
light gaieties of frivolous mirth and wantonness
which the courteous nature of Guyon may
suffer to play until they pass the bounds of
modesty.   (II. vi. 21.)   When, however, she
tried to win his heart from warlike enterprise
into dissolute delights of sense, Guyon

> " was wise, and warie of her will,
> And ever held his hand upon his hart :
> Yet would not seeme so rude, and thewed ill,
> As to despise so courteous seeming part,
> That gentle Ladie did to him impart,
> But fairely tempring fond desire subdewd,
> And ever her desired to depart."
>
> (II. vi. 26.)

The second trial of Guyon's temperance comes in the House of Mammon, where he triumphs over sensual desire in the form of covetousness. Mammon offers him mountains of gold, if he will but serve him (II. vii. 9) ; he tries to induce him to accept by saying that money is the one necessity to supply all the wants of man. (II. vii. 11.)   But Guyon answers :

> " Indeede (quoth he) through fowle intemperaunce,
> Frayle men are oft captiv'd to covetise."
>
> (II. vii. 15.)

When Mammon urges him to seat himself on the silver stool in the Garden of Proserpina, to rest awhile and eat of the golden fruit of the trees, —

> " All which he did, to doe him deadly fall
> In frayle intemperance through sinful bayt ; "

Guyon

> " was warie wise in all his way,
> And well perceived his deceiptfull sleight,

Ne suffred lust his safetie to betray;
So goodly did beguile the Guyler of the pray."

                                    (II. vii. 64.)

The culminating trial of the Knight's temperance is made in Acrasia's Bower of Bliss.
Acrasia typifies that form of beauty that allures
the senses with pleasure, but ruins the soul
with its poisonous delight. (II. i. 52, 53.) The
only fear that she and the inmates of her bower
have is

" wisedomes powre, and temperaunces might,
By which the mightiest things efforced bin."

                                    (II. xii. 43.)

During the passage to this place of delight,
and while he was within its precincts, Guyon
was able to withstand every assault of sensual
desire upon his soul. When the Palmer, speaking as reason dictated, told him that the piteous
cry of a woman in distress was only a deceitful
ruse to win him to harm —

" The knight was ruled, and the Boatman strayt
Held on his course with stayed stedfastnesse."

                                    (II. xii. 28, 29.)

Again, when Guyon's senses are "softly tickled"
by the rare melody of the mermaids, as it min-

gled with the strange harmony of the rolling
sea, he bids the boatman row easily.

> " But him the Palmer from that vanity,
>   With temperate advice discounselled,
>   That they it past."   (II. xii. 34.)

Even when Guyon began to lessen his pace at
the sight of the fair maidens sporting in the
lake, which kindled signs of lust in his countenance, his reason was able to resist.

> " On which when gazing him the Palmer saw,
>   He much rebukt those wandring eyes of his,
>   And counseld well, him forward thence did draw."
>   (II. xii. 69.)

He has now become so strong that he can
perform the great object of his adventures,
the destruction of the Bower of Bliss and the
capture of the enchantress, Acrasia. (II. xii.
83, 84.)

So powerful is the hold on Spenser's mind of
this Platonic conception of the nature of the
struggle in the soul striving to be temperate
that it colors even the Aristotelean doctrine of
the mean which is worked out in the episode of
Medina's castle. (II. ii. 13 *et seq.*) According to Aristotle temperance is a mean between

the excess and defect of pleasure. ("Nich. Ethics," III, 10.)   In Spenser, Medina is the mean ; her two sisters, Elissa and Perissa, are the defect and excess respectively.   (II. ii. 35, 36.)   Yet Spenser has colored the character of each in accordance with the Platonic division of the soul.   The three sisters are daughters of one sire by three different mothers ; that is, they are the three principles of the soul (the sire) ; namely, right reason (Medina), wrath or spirit (Elissa), and sensual desire (Perissa). Thus Spenser describes Elissa :

> " with bent lowring browes, as she would threat,
> She scould, and frownd with froward countenaunce ; "

(II. ii. 35.)

and Perissa

> " Full of disport, still laughing, loosely light,
>   And quite contrary to her sisters kind ;
>   No measure in her mood, no rule of right,
>   But poured out in pleasure and delight."

(II. ii. 36.)

So, too, in the description of the lovers of each, the presence of the two irrational principles is felt.   In Hudibras, the devoted Knight of Elissa —

> " not so good of deedes, as great of name,
> Which he by many rash adventures wan,

*   *   *   *   *

> More huge in strength, then wise in workes he was,
> And reason with foole-hardize over ran," —

(II. ii. 17.)

the angry impulse of the soul is reflected ; while
in Sans Loy, the lover of Perissa, who had
attempted to violate the purity of Una, —

> "The most unruly, and the boldest boy,
>   That ever warlike weapons menaged,
>   And to all lawlesse lust encouraged," —

(II. ii. 18.)

it is apparent that the appetitive element of the
soul is figured.   Temperance, then, according
to Spenser, is not the golden mean between the
excess and defect of pleasure, but between two
disturbing passions.

> "But temperance (said he) with golden squire
>   Betwixt them both can measure out a meane,
>   Neither to melt in pleasures whot desire,
>   Nor fry in hartlesse griefe and dolefull teene."

(II. i. 57.)

This struggle between the rational principle
and the irrational elements in the soul does not,
however, constitute temperance.   That virtue,
or rather that condition of all virtue, is the
harmony and order resulting in the soul after
reason has quieted the disturbing passions, and
is conceived by Plato as its very health or

beauty. "'Healthy,' as I conceive," says Socrates, "is the name which is given to the regular
order of the body, whence comes health and
every other bodily excellence. . . . And 'lawful' and 'law' are the names which are given
to the regular order and action of the soul,
and these make men lawful and orderly : —
and so we have temperance and justice."
("Gorgias," 504.)   The fruition of this idea
in Spenser's mind is noticeable in his manner
of speaking about temperance throughout his
poem.   Amavia had been able to win her husband back to the ways of purity through wise
handling and "faire governaunce." (II. i. 54.)
The Red Cross Knight mentions the "goodly
governaunce" of Guyon's life.   (II. i. 29.)
Spenser comments in an introductory stanza on
the Knight's demeanor in pleasures and pains :

> "And *Guyon* in them all shewes goodly maisteries."

The Knight and the Palmer move on in their
path of progress "in this faire wize," that is,
in the ways of temperance. (II. i. 34.) When
Archimago meets Guyon, he meets

> "Faire marching underneath a shady hill,
>   A goodly knight,"

*   *   *   *   *

> " His carriage was full comely and upright,
>   His countenaunce demure and temperate."
>
>   (II. i. 5, 6.)

The feeling of order is conveyed through the movements of Guyon's charger. The Palmer

> " ever with slow pace the knight did lead,
>   Who taught his trampling steed with equall steps to
>   tread."   (II. i. 7.)

Medina, when she welcomes Guyon to her castle, meets him

> " Faire marching forth in honorable wize."
>
>   (II. ii. 14.)

The clearest explanation, however, of Spenser's conception of temperance as the condition of the soul's excellence in the body is given in his reflection at the opening of the eleventh book of the second canto, which records the repulse of the bodily senses from the dwelling-place of Alma, or the soul. No war is so fierce as that of the passions with the soul.

> " But in a body, which doth freely yeeld
>   His partes to reasons rule obedient,
>   And letteth her that ought the scepter weeld,
>   All happy peace and goodly government
>   Is setled there in sure establishment;
>   There *Alma* like a virgin Queene most bright,
>   Doth florish in all beautie excellent:

And to her guestes doth bounteous banket dight,
Attempred goodly well for health and for delight.

(II. xi. 2.)

After this examination of Spenser's ideals of
holiness and temperance, it is clear why Platonism as a system of ethics is absent in the
remaining books of the "Faerie Queene." Spenser's avowed aim in his poem was "to fashion
a gentleman or noble person in vertuous and
gentle discipline." Since he conceives of life
as a constant warfare with inward and outward
foes, his method of presenting his thought is
to send each virtue on a journey during which
it is to perfect itself by overcoming the vices
to whose assaults it is especially liable. This
plan is carefully followed in the first two books.
The allegorical scheme is unbroken; the personages encountered by the Knights are objec-
tified states of their own spiritual consciousness.
In the remaining books, however, the allegorical scheme has well-nigh broken down; and
the poetic method is that of the romantic epic
of adventure in the manner of Ariosto. This
change was due very largely to the fact that
after Spenser had completed his first two books
he had exhausted the ethical teachings of

Plato ; and when he went on to his remaining books, he passed out of the sphere of virtue as taught by Plato into an essentially different realm of thought in which the graces of courtly accomplishment were dignified as virtues. He tried to treat these later virtues of chastity, friendship, justice, courtesy, and constancy as if they were coördinate with the virtues of holiness and temperance. But they fall into a distinct class by themselves. They are the ideals of conduct to be followed when man is acting in his purely social capacity as a member of society. They may be dignified as virtues, but can never be coördinate with the Platonic conception of virtue, which conceives of it not as an outward act, but as the very health of the soul when realizing, unhampered by any disturbing influences, its native impulses toward the good.

The difference between these two conceptions is strikingly illustrated by a comparison of Spenser's idea of justice with the Platonic notion. According to the English poet, justice is purely retributive, a dispensing of reward and punishment. The education of the Knight of Justice, Arthegal, by Astræa, is thus described :

" There she him taught to weigh both right and wrong
    In equall ballance with due recompence,
    And equitie to measure out along,
    According to the line of conscience,
    When so it needs with rigour to dispence."

(V. i. 7.)

In Plato, on the other hand, justice is the same
thing as temperance, an inward state of the
soul and the condition of any virtue. "But,"
says Socrates, "in reality justice was such as
we were describing, being concerned however
not with the outward man, but with the inward, which is the true self and concernment
of man : for the just man does not permit the
several elements within him to interfere with
one another, or any of them to do the work of
others, — he sets in order his own inner life,
and is his own master and his own law, and at
peace with himself ; and when he has bound
together the three principles within him . . .
and is no longer many, but has become one
entirely temperate and perfectly adjusted nature, then he proceeds to act . . . always
thinking and calling that which preserves and
coöperates with this harmonious condition, just
and good action, and the knowledge which presides over it, wisdom, and that which at any

time impairs this condition, he will call unjust action, and the opinion which presides over it ignorance." ("Republic," IV. 443.) Spenser did not attempt to incorporate this idea into his notion of justice ; he had already exhausted it in his second book, in his explanation of temperance. Nothing was left for him to do but to shift his mind from a conception of virtue as one, to an inferior notion of virtue as a manifold of personal graces. But in thus changing his idea, he destroyed the unity of his work. In his first two books he had explained how the soul could perfect itself in the full scope of its powers ; and in doing this he had taught the Platonic doctrines of a heavenly beauty and of temperance as the condition of virtue in the soul. Here lay the basic idea of his conception of a gentleman.

"But vertue's seat is deepe within the mynd,
  And not in outward shows, but inward thoughts defynd."
                    (VI., Introd., stz. 5.)

This idea, however, is not felt as the informing spirit of his books on courtesy and on friendship, but appears only in scattered reflections. In the later books the inferior conception of

virtue is the controlling idea, and Spenser has
failed to harmonize it with his earlier and finer
one.

III. CHASTITY

Although Platonism as a system of ethical
philosophy determined the structural unity of
the first two books of the " Faerie Queene " and
as a system ceases to be felt in the construction of
the later books, the purity of its ethical teaching is present throughout the entire work.
The truths of Platonism were a strong influence in moulding an ideal of noble love.
The cardinal doctrine of this ethical philosophy was that true beauty is to be found by
the soul only in moral ideas.   This conviction, which was so powerful in ennobling the
Christian conception of holiness, was carried
over into the realm of man's social relations,
and through the genius of Spenser made to
dignify the conception of human love, and to
inform with a profound spiritual truth the idea
of chastity in its broadest signification as the
purity of the soul.

The influence of the ethical conception of
beauty upon the subject of romantic love is

found in the work of Spenser. Although
Spenser's mind had a strong bent toward
philosophy, so that it could interpret the very
spirit of Plato's conception of wisdom and
temperance, it was still a mind in which the
genius of the poet was always uppermost. It
thus resulted that in him the teaching of the
beauty of moral ideas came to fruition in
ennobling the conception of human life by
an appreciation of the true beauty of woman's
inner nature, her womanhood, and by a conception of love that placed its source in the
reverent adoration of this spiritual beauty.

The exposition of the true inward beauty
of woman is found in the "Epithalamion" and
in a minor episode of the "Faerie Queene."
In the account of the dialectic, by which the
lover gains a sight of absolute beauty, Plato
has stated that at one stage the lover will
see that beauty of mind surpasses beauty of
outward form. Plato says, "In the next stage
he will consider that the beauty of the mind is
more honourable than the beauty of outward
form." ("Symposium," 210.) This idea lies at
the basis of Spenser's praise of beauty in the
"Epithalamion." In his marriage hymn he

dwells in exuberant Renaissance fashion upon
the physical perfections of the bride, each detail an object of delight to the senses.   The
sight of such beauty amazes the beholders.
But after this is done, Spenser draws attention
to the truth that, although these perfections
that are visible to the eye may daze the mind,
there is a higher beauty of soul which no eye
can see.   His admiration for the bride's beauty
is then caught up into a more lofty pitch and
blended with his love of her moral qualities.

" Tell me ye merchants daughters did ye see
　So fayre a creature in your towne before,
　So sweet, so lovely, and so mild as she,
　Adornd with beautyes grace and vertues store,
　Her goodly eyes lyke Saphyres shining bright,
　Her forehead yvory white,
　Her cheekes lyke apples which the sun hath rudded,
　Her lips lyke cherryes charming men to byte,
　Her brest lyke to a bowle of creame uncrudded,
　Her paps lyke lyllies budded,
　Her snowie necke lyke to a marble towre,
　And all her body like a pallace fayre,
　Ascending uppe with many a stately stayre,
　To honors seat and chastities sweet bowre.
　Why stand ye still ye virgins in amaze,
　Upon her so to gaze,
　Whiles ye forget your former lay to sing,
　To which the woods did answer and your eccho ring? "

" But if ye saw that which no eyes can see,
  The inward beauty of her lively spright,
  Garnisht with heavenly guifts of high degree,
  Much more then would ye wonder at that sight,
  And stand astonisht lyke to those which red
  Medusaes mazefull hed.
  There dwels sweet love and constant chastity,
  Unspotted fayth and comely womanhood,
  Regard of honour and mild modesty,
  There vertue raynes as Queene in royal throne,
  And giveth lawes alone.
  The which the base affections doe obay,
  And yeeld theyr services unto her will,
  Ne thought of things uncomely ever may
  Thereto approch to tempt her mind to ill.
  Had ye once seene these her celestial threasures,
  And unrevealed pleasures,
  Then would ye wonder and her prayses sing,
  That al the woods should answer and your echo ring."
                              (ll. 167–203.)

In the " Faerie Queene " there is a less elaborate example of this same appreciation of the
inward, unseen beauty of the soul.   The contrast is set up between the lively portrait of the
Faerie Queene on Guyon's shield and the actual
beauty of her person, and then extended to a
comparison of this with the beauty of her mind.
Arthur has asked Guyon who is the original
of the portrait he bears on his shield and has
chanced to notice its great liveliness.   Guyon

does not answer directly, but breaks out into
praise of the Queen's beauty. If a mere like-
ness appeals so strongly to Arthur, what must
he think when he beholds the glorious original ; and though this is fair, the beauty of her
mind, if he but knew it, would arouse great
wonder and pour infinite desire into his soul.

> " Faire Sir (said he) if in that picture dead
>   Such life ye read, and vertue in vaine shew,
>   What mote ye weene, if the trew lively-head
>   Of that most glorious visage ye did view?
>   But if the beautie of her mind ye knew,
>   That is her bountie, and imperiall powre,
>   Thousand times fairer then her mortall hew,
>   O how great wonder would your thoughts devoure,
>   And infinite desire into your spirite poure!"

(II. ix. 3.)

In the vision of this inward world of beauty
in woman's mind, so Spenser teaches, begins
the passion of love. In the "Phædrus" Plato
has analyzed it as a divine fury, and in his
account he emphasizes the feeling of reverence
with which the lover gazes upon the beauty
of the beloved, seeing in it the idea of pure
beauty which his soul has beheld in its pre-
natal existence. "But he," says Plato, "whose
initiation is recent, and who has been the spec-

tator of many glories in the other world, is
amazed when he sees any one having a godlike
face or any bodily form which is the expression
of divine beauty ; and at first a shudder runs
through him, and again the old awe steals over
him ; then looking upon the face of his beloved
as of a god he reverences him, and if he were
not afraid of being thought a downright madman, he would sacrifice to his beloved as
to the image of a god." (" Phædrus," 251.)
The habit of contemplating the beauty of the
beloved in reverent fear is characteristic of the
love which Arthegal feels for Britomart. So intimately acquainted was Spenser with Plato that
he caught the spirit of his worship of beauty.
Disguised as Britomart, the virgin Knight of
Chastity, was, in her panoply of armor, her
beauty was not the object of constant sight.
On three different occasions, however, when by
the removal of some portion of it her features
shine forth, the impression made by her beauty
is that of reverent adoration. When Arthegal
chances thus to behold her, the sight is so
awful that he hesitates to press his suit for her
love, and only after some time does he venture
to win her affections.

One occasion on which the spectators catch
a glimpse of Britomart's beauty occurs when
she unlaces her helmet. The sight of her golden
locks strikes all with amazement; and though
there is a mingled feeling of surprise and curi-
osity, due to the preconceived notion of her sex,
the feeling of amazement and adoration of her
beauty is expressly stated as consequent upon
this revelation.

" With that, her glistring helmet she unlaced;
    Which doft, her golden lockes, that were up bound
    Still in a knot, unto her heeles downe traced,
    And like a silken veile in compasse round
    About her backe and all her bodie wound;
    Like as the shining skie in summers night,
    What time the dayes with scorching heat abound,
    Is creasted all with lines of firie light,
That it prodigious seemes in common peoples sight.

" Such when those Knights and Ladies all about
    Beheld her, all were with amazement smit,
    And every one gan grow in secret dout
    Of this and that, according to each wit:

> *   *   *   *   *

" But that young Knight [Scudamour], which through
        her gentle deed
    Was to that goodly fellowship restor'd,
    Ten thousand thankes did yeeld her for her meed,
    And doubly overcommen, her ador'd."

                                (IV. i. 13, 14, 15.)

A second time when her beauty is revealed in greater fulness, the feeling of terror and amazement inspired is especially emphasized. The spectators are described as standing in mute astonishment, in worship of her divine beauty.

" Which whenas they beheld, they smitten were
　With great amazement of so wondrous sight,
　And each on other, and they all on her
　Stood gazing, as if suddein great affright
　Had them surprised.　At last avizing right,
　Her goodly personage and glorious hew,
　Which they so much mistooke, they tooke delight
　In their first errour, and yet still anew
With wonder of her beauty fed their hungry vew.

"Yet note their hungry vew be satisfide,
　But seeing still the more desir'd to see,
　And ever firmely fixed did abide
　In contemplation of divinitie."

(III. ix. 23, 24.)

In the fight between Britomart and Arthegal the sword of the latter cuts away a part of her ventayle, discovering to his view her beautiful face.　As he is about to raise his arm for a second blow, he is benumbed with fear, and, falling on his knee, he gazes upon her beauty with a true religious feeling of wonder.

" And as his hand he up againe did reare,
   Thinking to worke on her his utmost wracke,
   His powrelesse arme benumbd with secret feare
   From his revengefull purpose shronke abacke,
   And cruell sword out of his fingers slacke
   Fell downe to ground, as if the steele had sence,
   And felt some ruth, or sence his hand did lacke,
   Or both of them did thinke, obedience
   To doe to so divine a beauties excellence.

"And he himselfe long gazing thereupon
   At last fell humbly downe upon his knee,
   And of his wonder made religion,
   Weening some heavenly goddesse he did see,
   Or else unweeting, what it else might bee;
   And pardon her besought his errour frayle,
   That had done outrage in so high degree;
   Whilest trembling horrour did his sense assayle,
   And made ech member quake, and manly hart to
       quayle."

(IV. vi. 21, 22.)

With this vision of the resplendent beauty
of chastity begins Arthegal's love for Britomart.
It has been pointed out by critics that the love
episode between Britomart and Arthegal was
a suggestion — so far as plot goes — which
Spenser found in Ariosto's account of the love
of Ruggiero and Bradamante in the " Orlando
Furioso." [1]   But the great difference in the

[1] Cf. Pub. of Mod. Lang. Ass. of Amer., 1897, p. 177,
"Spenser's Imitations from Ariosto."

poets appears in the contrast of the passionate
love of beauty revealed in Spenser's poem with
the superficial delights of love as explained in
Ariosto.   As has already been seen, Platonism
as a system of ethics disappears from the
" Faerie Queene " after the second book ; but
so deeply had Spenser been impressed with
the worship of beauty characteristic of Plato's
manner, that when he came to recount the his-
tory of the passion of love, in his Knight of
Justice, for his heroine, Chastity, he centred
attention upon the feeling of awe and reverence inspired by the beauty of chastity, and
intimated the sobering effect of this vision upon
the behavior of the lover.   He found nothing
like this in the " Orlando Furioso."   The love
episode in Ariosto is thus briefly described :

> " Rogero looks on Bradamant, and she
>   Looks on Rogero in profound surprise
>   That for so many days that witchery
>   Had so obscured her altered mind and eyes.
>   Rejoiced, Rogero clasps his lady free,
>   Crimsoning with deeper than the rose's dyes,
>   And his fair love's first blossoms, while he clips
>   The gentle damsel, gathers from her lips.
>
> " A thousand times they their embrace renew,
>   And closely each is by the other prest ;

> While so delightful are these lovers two,
> Their joys are ill contained within their breast."
>
> (xxii. 32, 33.)

Here is only the note of delight. In Spenser, however, the dread awe aroused by Britomart's beauty restrains the passionate utterance of the lover, and only after some time has elapsed, during which the two have rested from the fatigues of their combat, does Arthegal dare to make suit to Britomart's affections, —

> " Yet durst he not make love so suddenly,
>   Ne thinke th' affection of her hart to draw
> From one to other so quite contrary."
>
> (IV. vi. 33.)

The training afforded by the philosophy of Plato in the realization of the true moral value of beauty has a somewhat different result in the work of Milton. Owing to his preconceived notion of the moral inferiority of woman, Milton does not permit his mind to dwell upon the vision of beauty to be seen in her, as Spenser's chivalric impulses have led him to do ; but in Milton the flowering of Platonic thought is found in a certain conception of chastity, which teaches that love begins and ends only in the soul. And yet the deep sense of beauty which

he has, asserts itself at times even in spite
of his prejudices ; consequently in his work
there is a wavering of mind between the conviction that woman's beauty cannot be the
expression of the beauty of a moral order, since
she is the moral inferior of man, and the more
chivalric notion that in her beauty lies the
inspiration of the soul to know goodness.

In Milton the love of beauty is the conscious
activity of a contemplative mind rather than
the pouring out of the soul's passion in reverent adoration.   About Spenser beauty lies
as a golden splendour streaming from the hidden world of the moral nature ; whenever it
shines upon the lover's sight, it at once moves
him to silent adoration.   In Milton, on the
other hand, beauty is an idea to be known in
the soul by him who seeks for it among the
beautiful objects of the world of sense ; its
pursuit is an intellectual quest of a philosophic
mind.   Writing to his friend, Charles Diodati,
he says : " What besides God has resolved concerning me I know not, but this at least : *He
has instilled into me, at all events, a vehement love
of the beautiful.*   Not with so much labour as the
fables have it, is Ceres said to have sought her

daughter Proserpine, as I am wont day and night to seek for this *idea of the beautiful* (hanc τοῦ καλοῦ ἰδέαν) through all the forms and faces of things (*for many are the shapes of things divine*), and to follow it leading me on as with certain assured traces." [1]

The expression of this love of beauty is found in Milton's Satan. Abiding beneath the wreck of his moral character, in spite of the perversion of a malicious will, there remain in Satan a deep sense of beauty and a contemplative love of it for its moral quality. In a speech addressed to Christ in "Paradise Regained" Satan himself confesses this one conviction of his soul. The contemplative love of the beauty of goodness and virtue is the very condition of his soul's existence. Thus he says :

> "Though I have lost,
> Much lustre of my native brightness, lost
> To be beloved of God, I have not lost
> To love, at least contemplate and admire,
> What I see excellent in good, or fair,
> Or virtuous ; I should so have lost all sense."
>
> (I. 377–382.)

The honesty of this confession is not impugned by Christ, although he exposes the hollow in-

[1] Masson, Life of Milton, I. 600.

sincerity of the rest of Satan's speech in which these lines occur.

And Satan lives up to his confession. The power of moral goodness to hold his mind's thought by its beauty is seen in his behavior in the Garden of Eden. He had reached this place in pursuit of his revenge to ruin the happy pair. As he gazes upon the beauties of the garden,

> " where the Fiend
> Saw undelighted all delight, all kind
> Of living creatures, new to sight and strange," —
> (IV. 285–287.)

he at last catches sight of Adam and Eve, in whom

> " The image of their glorious Maker shone,
> Truth, wisdom, sanctitude severe and pure."
> (IV. 292–293.)

On these he stands gazing until evening, and at last breaks out into an expression of the love which this vision of their beauty has aroused in him :

> " the sun,
> Declined, was hasting now with prone career
> To the Ocean Isles, and in the ascending scale
> Of Heaven the stars that usher evening rose :
> When Satan, still in gaze, as first he stood,
> Scarce thus at length failed speech recovered sad : —

'O Hell ! what do mine eyes with grief behold ?
Into our room of bliss thus high advanced
Creatures of other mould — Earth-born perhaps,
Not spirits, yet to Heavenly Spirits bright
Little inferior — whom my thoughts pursue
With wonder, and could love ; so lively shines
In them divine resemblance, and such grace
The hand that formed them on their shape hath poured.'"
                          (IV. 352–365.)

At another time Satan is occupied in contemplating beauty, but it is the beauty he sees in
Eve alone.   Milton's treatment of the episode is
characteristic of that wavering of his mind between the two impulses — one to worship beauty,
and the other to teach that woman is the inferior
of man.   The later conviction is expressed in
Adam's words to Raphael :

" For well I understand in the prime end
  Of Nature her the inferior, in the mind
  And inward faculties, which most excel ;
  In outward also her resembling less
  His image who made both, and less expressing
  The character of that dominion given
  O'er other creatures."
                          (VIII. 540–546.)

Thus Eve confesses that in Adam's beauty, and
not in the image of her own soft feminine grace,
does she
                          " see
  How beauty is excelled by manly grace
  And wisdom, which alone is truly fair."
                          (IV. 489–491.)

Yet in the presence of Eve's beauty Satan stands lost in contemplation, made for one moment good.

> "Such pleasure took the Serpent to behold
> This flowery plat, the sweet recess of Eve
> Thus early, thus alone. Her heavenly form
> Angelic, but more soft and feminine,
> Her graceful innocence, her every air
> Of gesture or least action, overawed
> His malice, and with rapine sweet bereaved
> His fierceness of the fierce intent it brought.
> That space the Evil One abstracted stood
> From his own evil, and for the time remained
> Stupidly good, of enmity disarmed,
> Of guile, of hate, of envy, of revenge."
>
> (IX. 455–466.)

Even here the idea of the inferiority of Eve's beauty enters into the description; but a few lines below it makes itself even more strongly felt. Because her beauty is without its power to inspire awe and terror, Satan reasons that she is the proper one to tempt.

> "Then let me not let pass
> Occasion which now smiles. Behold alone
> The Woman, opportune to all attempts —
> Her husband, for I view far round, not nigh,
> Whose higher intellectual more I shun.
>
>   *   *   *   *   *
>
> She fair, divinely fair, fit love for Gods,
> Not terrible, though terror be in love

And beauty, not approached by stronger hate,
Hate stronger under show of love well feigned."

(IX. 479–492.)

In this contemplative love of beauty there is
present as a noticeable element the consciousness in the poet's mind of the moral significance
of beauty.   In Spenser's description of the first
meeting of Calidore with Pastorella, however,
the contemplative love of beauty so absorbs the
power of the soul that the lover and the poet
are oblivious to every other thought and silently
gaze upon the beauty of form present to their
eyes.   Calidore sees Pastorella on a little hillock
surrounded by maidens, she lovelier than all.

"So stood he still long gazing thereupon,
  Ne any will had thence to move away,
  Although his quest were farre afore him gon;
  But after he had fed, yet did he stay,
  And sate there still, untill the flying day
  Was farre forth spent."

(VI. ix. 12.)

So Satan stands before the happy pair in Paradise.   His will toward them is far otherwise
than Calidore's toward Pastorella ; but his contemplative love of their beauty is one in spirit
with the youthful lover's.

The most characteristic side of Milton's
idealism, however, is revealed in his teaching
of the doctrine of chastity as the purity of the
soul. In the defence of his own life which he
made in "An Apology for Smectymnuus," he
acknowledges an important debt in his education to the teaching of Platonic philosophy.
"Thus, from the laureat fraternity of poets,"
he says, "riper years and the ceaseless round
of study and reading led me to the shady spaces
of philosophy ; but chiefly to the divine vol-
umes of Plato, and his equal Xenophon : where,
if I should tell ye what I learnt of chastity and
love, I mean that which is truly so, whose
charming cup is only virtue, which she bears
in her hand to those who are worthy . . . and
how the first and chiefest office of love begins
and ends in the soul, producing those happy
twins of her divine generation, knowledge and
virtue : with such abstracted sublimities as
these, it might be worth your listening, readers,
as I may one day hope to have ye in a still
time, when there shall be no chiding." [1] Milton was the only poet of his time who was able
to conceive of chastity as an "abstracted sub-

[1] Milton, Prose Works, I. 225.

limity," known in and by the soul. In his
treatment of this theme, there are two phases :
one in which the enthusiasm of Milton asserts
itself in a positive way, and the other a conviction of maturer experience, in which sin is
explained negatively in its relation to the
soul's purity.

The fundamental idea of Plato on which
Milton built his doctrine of chastity is the one
taught in the " Phædo," that every experience of the soul gained through the medium
of the senses tends to degrade the soul's pure
essence into the grosser, corporeal form of the
body. " And were we not saying long ago,"
says Socrates, " that the soul, when using the
body as an instrument of perception, that is
to say, when using the sense of sight or hearing or some other sense (for the meaning of
perceiving through the body is perceiving
through the senses) — were we not saying
that the soul too is then dragged by the
body into the region of the changeable, and
wanders and is confused; the world spins
round her, and she is like a drunkard, when
she touches change?" ("Phædo," 79.) This
appears in the " Comus " in a modified form,

and constitutes the basis for Milton's conception of sin in "Paradise Lost."   In the masque
the idea is plainly stated by the Elder Brother
in his explanation of the doctrine of chastity;
and its workings are seen in the effect of the
magic potion of Comus upon all who drink it.

> " But, when lust,
> By unchaste looks, loose gestures, and foul talk,
> But most by lewd and lavish act of sin,
> Lets in defilement to the inward parts,
> The soul grows clotted by contagion,
> Imbodies, and imbrutes, till she quite lose
> The divine property of her first being.
> Such are those thick and gloomy shadows damp
> Oft seen in charnel-vaults, and sepulchres,
> Lingering and sitting by a new-made grave,
> As loath to leave the body that it loved;
> And linked itself by carnal sensualty
> To a degenerate and degraded state." [1]
>
> (ll. 463–475.)

This idea, thus stated, is represented symboli-
cally in the disfigurement which the magic

---

[1] ll. 470–475 are taken from " Phædo," 81 : " And this corporeal element, my friend, is heavy and weighty and earthy,
and is that element of sight by which a soul is depressed
and dragged down again into the visible world, because she
is afraid of the invisible and of the world below — prowling
about tombs and sepulchres, near which, as they tell us, are
seen certain ghostly apparitions of souls which have not departed pure, but are cloyed with sight, and therefore visible."

liquor of Comus works in the divine character of the soul visible in the countenance.

> "Soon as the potion works, their human count'nance,
>   The express resemblance of the gods, is changed
>   Into some brutish form of wolf or bear,
>   Or ounce or tiger, hog, or bearded goat,
>   All other parts remaining as they were.
>   And they, so perfect is their misery,
>   Not once perceive their foul disfigurement,
>   But boast themselves more comely than before,
>   And all their friends and native home forget,
>   To roll with pleasure in a sensual sty."
>
> (ll. 68–77.)

The opposition indicated in the Platonic doctrine between the senses and the soul is carried over by Milton in his description of the trial undergone by the spirit of him who strives to be chaste. In Plato the fundamental idea is somewhat different from Milton's; for Plato is concerned with the problem of the attainment by the soul of pure knowledge, and he means by sense knowledge not sensuality in the restricted moral signification of that word, but in the broader signification of all experience gained through all the senses. Milton, however, places a narrow interpretation upon the doctrine of Plato. This is evident in his description of

the attempt made by Comus to allure The Lady
to sensual indulgence.

Comus endeavors twice to overpower The
Lady. He tries to tempt her to impurity of
conduct, and also seeks to blind her judgment
through the power of sense illusion. In this
second trial there may be seen the influence of
the Platonic notion of sense knowledge destroy-
ing the soul's purity ; the first trial contains
the more narrow application of the idea of un-
chastity. Milton himself calls attention to the
greater similarity of Comus to his mother, Circe,
the enchantress of men's minds, than to Bacchus,
the god of wine. He is

> "a son
> Much like his father, but his mother more."
>
> (ll. 56, 57.)

In keeping with his character he tries to entice
The Lady to drink his magic potion. He reminds her that about him are all the pleasures
that fancy can beget ; he praises the marvellous
efficacy of his elixir in stirring joy within ; and
pleads with her not to be cruel to the dainty
limbs that were given for gentle usage.

> "See, here be all the pleasures
> That fancy can beget on youthful thoughts,

> When the fresh blood grows lively, and returns
> Brisk as the April buds in primrose season.
> And first behold this cordial julep here,
> That flames and dances in his crystal bounds,
> With spirits of balm and fragrant syrups mixed.
> Not that Nepenthes which the wife of Thone
> In Egypt gave to Jove-born Helena
> Is of such power to stir up joy as this,
> To life so friendly, or so cool to thirst.
> Why should you be so cruel to yourself,
> And to those dainty limbs, which Nature lent
> For gentle usage, and soft delicacy?
> But you invert the covenants of her trust,
> And harshly deal, like an ill borrower,
> With that which you received on other terms,
> Scorning the unexempt condition
> By which all mortal frailty must subsist,
> Refreshment after toil, ease after pain,
> That have been tired all day without repast,
> And timely rest have wanted.   But, fair virgin,
> This will restore all soon."
>
> (ll. 668–689.)

To this argument The Lady replies simply that no real pleasure can result from mere physical gratification, but only from the enjoyment of the moral quality of goodness.   Thus she says to Comus :

> "I would not taste thy treasonous offer.   None
> But such as are good men can give good things;
> And that which is not good is not delicious
> To a well-governed and wise appetite."
>
> (ll. 702–705.)

But when Comus reveals the more subtle
trait of his nature, the response which The
Lady makes rises to the height of the threaten-
ing danger.   The Circean strain in his character is his power of deceiving the soul through
sense illusion, and his insidious desire to win
his way into the hearts of men by courteous
words and gay rhetoric.   Thus, when he first
is conscious of the approach of The Lady, he
says :

> " Thus I hurl
> My dazzling spells into the spongy air,
> Of power to cheat the eye with blear illusion,
> And give it false presentments."
>
> (ll. 153–156.)

The effect of this sense witchery is seen in the
forebodings of The Lady's fancy and in the hal-
lucinations that haunt her mind as she comes
within the range of its spells.   She says :

> " A thousand fantasies
> Begin to throng into my memory,
> Of calling shapes, and beckoning shadows dire,
> And airy tongues that syllable men's names
> On sands and shores and desert wildernesses."
>
> (ll. 205–209.)

When Comus, then, begins to practise the more
dangerous art of this witchery, acting in accordance with his confession of his manner, —

> " under fair pretence of friendly ends,
> And well-placed words of glozing courtesy,
> Baited with reasons not unplausible," —
>
> (ll. 160–162.)

she responds to the attack with an account
of the great power of chastity.   Only because
she sees that he is trying to deceive her judgment does she deign to answer him.

> " I had not thought to have unlocked my lips
> In this unhallowed air, but that this juggler
> Would think to charm my judgment, as mine eyes,
> Obtruding false rules pranked in reason's garb."
>
> (ll. 756–759.)

She then intimates the power which the doctrine of chastity has to overcome Comus, and
states that, should she attempt to unfold it, the
enthusiasm of her soul would be such as to
overwhelm him and his magic structures.

> " Enjoy your dear wit, and gay rhetoric,
> That hath so well been taught her dazzling fence ;
> Thou art not fit to hear thyself convinced.
> Yet, should I try, the uncontrollèd worth
> Of this pure cause would kindle my rapt spirits
> To such a flame of sacred vehemence
> That dumb things would be moved to sympathize,
> And the brute Earth would lend her nerves, and shake,
> Till all thy magic structures, reared so high,
> Were shattered into heaps o'er thy false head."
>
> (ll. 790–799.)

This vehemence of moral enthusiasm in Milton is due to the conception of chastity as an "abstracted sublimity." He learned it, he says, in his study of Platonic philosophy ; but the teaching of it as a positive doctrine applied to human conduct is his own contribution, and strikes the characteristic note of his idealism. In Plato he found only the suggestion of this teaching. It lay in that idea of the "Phædo," already explained, of the destruction of the soul's purity through sense knowledge. Milton's imagination, working upon this idea, transformed it in a way peculiar to himself alone. The pure soul, according to his belief, has power in itself to change the body to its own pure essence. The conversion of body to soul, however, is not a tenet of Platonic philosophy in any phase. It was the working in Milton of that tendency, visible throughout the poetry of the seventeenth century, to assert the primacy of the soul in life — an attempt which was made by the metaphysical poets especially in their treatment of love.

The statement of this theory of chastity is explained in "Comus," and its quickening influence is felt in the very manner in which Milton

refers to it. Before the Elder Brother recounts
the effect of lust upon the soul he explains the
hidden power of chastity.

> " So dear to Heaven is saintly chastity
>   That, when a soul is found sincerely so,
>   A thousand liveried angels lackey her,
>   Driving far off each thing of sin and guilt,
>   And in clear dream and solemn vision
>   Tell her of things that no gross ear can hear;
>   Till oft converse with heavenly habitants
>   Begin to cast a beam on the outward shape,
>   The unpolluted temple of the mind,
>   And turns it by degrees to the soul's essence,
>   Till all be made immortal."
>
> (ll. 453–463.)

This is the "abstracted sublimity" which The
Lady refers to when she addresses Comus. It
is a notion, a mystery, which he, standing for
the purely sensual instincts of man, cannot
apprehend. She tells him :

> " Thou hast nor ear, nor soul, to apprehend
>   The sublime notion and high mystery
>   That must be uttered to unfold the sage
>   And serious doctrine of Virginity;
>   And thou art worthy that thou shouldst not know
>   More happiness than this thy present lot."
>
> (ll. 784–789.)

So powerfully, indeed, has the vision of beauty
described in the " Phædrus " and the " Sym-

posium " affected Milton's own imagination that
he visualizes chastity much as Plato does an
idea; it is an idea not only known to the
mind, but thrilling the imagination with its
beauty. When The Lady is at first conscious
of the power of Comus's magic to disturb her
mind with foreboding fancies, she invokes
faith, hope, and chastity. The first two are
seen as personages, but chastity only as a pure,
unblemished form.

> " O, welcome, pure-eyed Faith, white-handed Hope,
> Thou hovering angel girt with golden wings,
> And thou unblemished form of Chastity !
> I see ye visibly."
>   (ll. 213–216.)

The directness of this vision is like that of the
soul in the " Phædrus " when it sees the flash-
ing beauty of the beloved, " which," says Plato,
" when the charioteer [the soul] sees, his
memory is carried to the true beauty, whom he
beholds in company with Modesty like an image
placed upon a holy pedestal." (" Phædrus,"
254.)

It is in the vision of this holy beauty as a
lost possession of the soul that the deadly pang
of sin lies. In Milton's later work there is no
reference to the power of the chaste soul to

change the body to its own pure essence ; but
his mind still holds to the power of sin to dim
the soul's lustre. This is strikingly exemplified
in the character of Satan's reflection on his faded
glory. The one keen regret that he feels, in
spite of his indomitable will, is occasioned by
the thought that by reason of sinning his form
has lost the beauty of its original goodness.
Throughout " Paradise Lost " there is repeated
emphasis upon the faded lustre of Satan's form.
The very first words that fall from Satan's lips,
in his speech to Beelzebub, as the two lay rolling in the fiery gulf, draw our attention to the
great change in their outward forms.

> " To whom the Arch-Enemy,
> And thence in Heaven called Satan, with bold words
> Breaking the horrid silence, thus began : —
>   ' If thou beest he — but Oh how fallen ! how changed
> From him ! — who, in the happy realms of light,
> Clothed with transcendent brightness, didst outshine
> Myriads, though bright.' "

(I. 81–87.)

And then, as Satan proceeds, his mind is directed to his own departed glory.

> " Yet not for those [*i.e.* the force of the Almighty's arms]
>   Nor what the potent Victor in his rage
>   Can else inflict, do I repent, or change,

Though changed in outward lustre, that fixed mind,
And high disdain from sense of injured merit."

(I. 94–98.)

In his address to the Sun Satan expresses his hatred of that bright light because it brings to remembrance the more glorious state from which he fell.

"O thou that, with surpassing glory crowned,
   Look'st from thy sole dominion like the god
   Of this new World — at whose sight all the stars
   Hide their diminished heads — to thee I call,
   But with no friendly voice, and add thy name,
   O Sun, to tell thee how I hate thy beams,
   That bring to my remembrance from what state
   I fell, how glorious once above thy sphere."

(IV. 32–39.)

When the moral significance of this change in his form flashes through his mind, Satan then suffers the deepest regret that could come to him. The episode in which he learns the true effect of his sin is his encounter with the angels, Ithuriel and Zephon. These two have found him "squat like a toad" at the ear of Eve, trying to work upon her mind while she sleeps. At the touch of Ithuriel's spear Satan springs up in his real form. Ithuriel then asks which of the rebel angels he may be. The lofty pride of Satan is touched to the quick.

" ' Know ye not, then,' said Satan, filled with scorn,
  ' Know ye not me? Ye knew me once no mate
  For you, there sitting where ye durst not soar!
  Not to know me argues yourselves unknown,
  The lowest of your throng.' "

(IV. 827–831.)

Zephon, however, points out that Satan should
not think that he may still be known, as he was
in heaven, by the brightness of his form; for
his glory departed when he rebelled, and now
resembles his sin and place of doom.

" Think not, revolted Spirit, thy shape the same,
  Or undiminished brightness, to be known
  As when thou stood'st in Heaven upright and pure.
  That glory then, when thou no more wast good,
  Departed from thee; and thou resemblest now
  Thy sin and place of doom obscure and foul."

(IV. 835–840.)

At this thought Satan stands abashed. Lover
of the beautiful as he is, he now experiences the
pang of its loss in his own life.

" So spake the Cherub; and his grave rebuke,
  Severe in youthful beauty, added grace
  Invincible. Abashed the Devil stood,
  And felt how awful goodness is, and saw
  Virtue in her shape how lovely — saw, and pined
  His loss; but chiefly to find here observed
  His lustre visibly impaired; yet seemed
  Undaunted."

(IV. 844–851.)

In Milton, then, whether his mind dwells on chastity or on the consciousness of sin's effect on the soul, it is to the vision of a world of moral beauty that at last it mounts.

The relation of these ideals of holiness, temperance, and chastity to the Christian doctrine of grace, which finds a place in the works of these English poets, can now be clearly seen. The ideals of conduct are essentially moral ideals, and in the attainment of them the soul lives its fullest life. " The being who possesses good always, everywhere, and in all things," says Socrates in the " Philebus " (60), "has the most perfect sufficiency." According to Plato the soul may realize perfect sufficiency of itself, it is self-sufficient ; but Christian theology taught the necessity of a heavenly grace for man to work out his own salvation. The two ideals are thus distinct ; and though the English poets incorporate both in their work, the line of cleavage is distinctly visible, and the doctrine of grace plays no more than a formal part in their exposition of the soul's growth. In the "Faerie Queene" and in " Comus " Platonic idealism triumphs over Christian theology.

In Spenser the adventures of Arthur, in

whom heavenly grace is commonly recognized, have no moral significance in the progress of the Knight aided by him toward the realization of virtue. Arthur frees the Red Cross Knight from Orgoglio and Duessa, but the Red Cross Knight is, morally speaking, the same man after he is freed as before ; the adventure of Arthur answers to no change significant in the moral order of his life as this is revealed in holiness. The realization of holiness as an intimate experience of the soul is achieved only after the Knight's training on the Mount of Heavenly Contemplation, which follows all his preceding discipline in the Christian graces; for this has left him a "man of earth." In the legend of temperance the efficacy of grace is no more vital, and what is more, it is an intrusion upon the moral order ; it makes the soul untrue to itself and all that we know of her. The logic of Guyon's inner life did not require that Arthur should come to his rescue after he had shown his ability to remain temperate under strong emotion and in the presence of wantonness and covetousness. His swoon at the end of the seventh canto has no more meaning than mere bodily fatigue after toil; morally, Guyon should have been only the stronger for his past victories over his passions. Arthur's entrance at the eighth canto, consequently, is not required : Spenser is only paralleling in his second book Arthur's advent in the eighth canto of his first.

Similarly in " Comus." When the younger brother inquires what that power which The Lady possesses to keep herself unspotted in the presence of lust may be, if it is not the strength of heaven, his elder companion replies :

> " I mean that too, but yet a hidden strength,
> Which, if Heaven gave it, may be termed her own.
> 'Tis chastity, my brother, chastity."
>
> (ll. 418–420.)

So The Lady herself witnesses, when in the great crisis of her life she appeals to faith, hope, and chastity; *if need were*, she is confident that heaven would send an angel to her defence.

> " O, welcome, pure-eyed Faith, white-handed Hope,
> Thou hovering angel, girt with golden wings,
> And thou unblemished form of Chastity !
> I see ye visibly, and now believe
> That He, the Supreme Good, to whom all things ill
> Are but as slavish officers of vengeance,
> Would send a glistering guardian, if need were,
> To keep my life and honour unassailed."
>
> (ll. 212–220.)

And the Guardian Spirit, in whose parting words is found the moral of the poem, explains the same idea of the self-sufficiency of the virtuous soul.

> " Mortals, that would follow me,
> Love Virtue; she alone is free.
> She can teach ye how to climb
> Higher than the sphery chime;
> Or, if Virtue feeble were,
> Heaven itself would stoop to her."
>
> (ll. 1018–1023.)

The theological doctrine of grace, although maintained as a part of an intellectual scheme of thought, did not enter into the inward life of Spenser's and Milton's work. So sensitive were they to the power of beauty that nothing could come between it and the soul. To Milton beauty wore an invincible grace, before which all must give way. Satan recognized this when he was confronted by the angel, Zephon.

> " So spake the Cherub; and his grave rebuke,
> Severe in youthful beauty, added grace
> Invincible."
>
> (IV. 844–846.)

Nothing was more natural, then, than that such a mind feeding upon Plato's thought and learning its great lesson of wisdom, that it alone is truly fair, should conceive virtue panoplied in all the might of beauty. He thus could teach in his " Comus " " the sun-clad power of chastity " :

> "She that has that is clad in complete steel,
> And, like a quivered nymph with arrows keen,
> May trace huge forests, and unharboured heaths,
> Infamous hills, and sandy perilous wilds,
> Where, through the sacred rays of chastity,
> No savage fierce, bandite, or mountaineer,
> Will dare to soil her virgin purity."
>
> (ll. 421–427.)

In Spenser beauty is not thus militant. When the Red Cross Knight, eager to enter the Cave of Error (I. i. 12), says to Una, confident in his power,

> "Virtue gives her selfe light, through darkenesse for to wade,"

Una cautions him to stay his step while there yet is time. (I. i. 13.) But it is just as true in Spenser as in Milton, that beauty is an unerring guide in life. Spenser responded to it because he felt most deeply the power of the soul's affinity for it. Throughout his work the influence of beauty upon man is constantly present. Even though at times he seems to be drawn to it by the subtlety of its appeal to the sense alone, he makes it very evident that true beauty can be found in the soul only in its habits of virtuous life.   Thus the witch Duessa, when stripped of her alluring beauty, is revolting in her hideousness (I. ii. 40; II. i. 22), and Acrasia's beauty only poisons the souls of her lovers.   (II. i. 54.)   Beauty that is nothing but a mere witchery of the sense disappears into thin air when confronted by virtue in her beauty.   This is the lesson taught in the vanishing of the false Florimell when the true is placed beside her.   (V. iii. 25.)   The power of this affinity of the soul for beauty, mysterious as it is real, which Spenser's work reveals, is conveyed in a question from Sidney's "Arcadia," where the spirit of the "Phædrus" is all present.   "Did ever mans eye looke thorough love upon the majesty of vertue, shining through beauty, but that he became (as it well became him) a captive?"[1]

[1] Lib. 3. fol. 313 recto.

CHAPTER II

THEORY OF LOVE

I. HEAVENLY LOVE

HEAVENLY love, as conceived in the poetry of the sixteenth and seventeenth centuries, refers to two distinct experiences. By this term the poets meant either the love known in the soul for the realities of the unseen world or the love which God had shown to man in his creation and preservation, and which man could experience through the indwelling of God's spirit within him. In the explanation of the nature of these two experiences the teaching of Platonism played a very important part, directing the course of that love of man for heavenly things, and accounting for the presence of love in the Godhead.

To the discussion of the latter of these subjects Platonism was able to offer two conceptions, in which a rational explanation of God's love as revealed in the creation could be found;

67

one presenting the highest reality as beauty, the other as the good. The first conception was present in its theory of love. In the "Symposium" Plato had taught that love was a desire of birth in beauty, and that the highest love was a desire of birth in beauty absolute, the ultimate principle of all beauty. ("Symposium," 206, 211–212.) Christianity, on the other hand, had taught that God is love. By identifying the absolute beauty of Plato with God, and by applying the Platonic conception of the birth of love to this Christian conception of God as love, God Himself was understood as enjoying his own beauty, thus begetting beings like to it in fairness. In Spenser's "Hymne of Heavenly Love," this idea forms the first division of the poem which treats of the love of God. (ll. 25–122.) At first God is conceived as living in Himself in love.

> " Before this worlds great frame, in which al things
>   Are now containd, found any being place,
>   Ere flitting Time could wag his eyas wings
>   About that mightie bound, which doth embrace
>   The rolling Spheres, and parts their houres by space,
>   That high eternall powre, which now doth move
>   In all these things, mov'd in it selfe by love."
>   (ll. 25–31.)

Loving itself, this Power brought forth, first
the Son.

> "It lov'd it selfe, because it selfe was faire;
> (For faire is lov'd;) and of it selfe begot
> Like to it selfe his eldest sonne and heire,
> Eternall, pure, and voide of sinfull blot."
>
> (ll. 32–35.)

After the creation of the Son God begets the
angels in His beauty.

> "Yet being pregnant still with powrefull grace,
> And full of fruitfull love, that loves to get
> Things like himselfe, and to enlarge his race,
> His second brood though not in powre so great,
> Yet full of beautie, next he did beget
> An infinite increase of Angels bright,
> All glistring glorious in their Makers light."
>
> (ll. 53–59.)

After the fall of the angels God finally creates
man.

> "Such he him made, that he resemble might
> Himselfe, as mortall thing immortall could;
> Him to be Lord of every living wight,
> He made by love out of his owne like mould,
> In whom he might his mightie selfe behould:
> For love doth love the thing belov'd to see,
> That like it selfe in lovely shape may bee."
>
> (ll. 116–122.)

The second conception of the highest reality
as the good is used in a more general way to

explain the reason of creation. In the "Timæus" the Maker of the universe is conceived as creating the world in goodness. "Let me tell you," says Timæus, "why the creator made this world of generation. He was good, and the good can never have any jealousy of anything. And being free from jealousy, he desired that all things should be as like himself as they could be." ("Timæus," 29.) In Henry More the idea is expressed in the closing canto of his "Psychathanasia," where he is accounting for the creation. (III. 4.) He has words of bitter denunciation for those who teach that God created the world merely as a manifestation of His power, His will. (III. iv. 22.) He maintains the Platonic teaching.

"When nothing can to Gods own self accrew,
  Who's infinitely happy; sure the end
  Of this creation simply was to shew
  His flowing goodnesse, which he doth out send
  Not for himself; for nought can him amend;
  But to his creature doth his good impart,
  This infinite *Good* through all the world doth wend
  To fill with heavenly blisse each willing heart.
  So the free Sunne doth 'light and 'liven every part."
                                        (III. iv. 16.)

So closely allied in the English poets are the teachings of Platonism with the devotional

spirit of Christian love that in the same man
and even in the same experience the thought
can pass most naturally from a conception of
Christ's love for God, as absolute beauty, to a
subjective treatment of it as a personal experience. Thus in George Herbert's lyric, " Love,"
the invocation is to the love of Christ for
God springing from His imperishable beauty;
but in the second division of the poem this
love has become a refining fire that can burn
all lusts within the soul and enable it to see
Him.

> " Immortall Love, author of this great frame,
>   Sprung from that beauty which can never fade,
>   How hath man parcel'd out Thy glorious name,
>   And thrown it in that dust which Thou hast made.
>
>   *   *   *   *   *
>   " Immortall Heat, O let Thy greater flame
>   Attract the lesser to it; let those fires
>   Which shall consume the world first make it tame,
>   And kindle in our hearts such true desires
>   As may consume our lusts, and make Thee way :
>   Then shall our hearts pant Thee, then shall our brain
>   All her invention on Thine altar lay,
>   And there in hymnes send back Thy fire again.
>
>   " Our eies shall see Thee, which before saw dust —
>   Dust blown by Wit, till that they both were blinde :
>   Thou shalt recover all Thy goods in kinde,
>   Who wert disseizèd by usurping lust."

The earlier conception of heavenly love, as related to absolute beauty, is not, however, the more important of the two themes of this poetry. From the very nature of the love itself, although it could be described in accordance with certain Platonic conceptions, it could not be the subject of a personal treatment; it gave no sufficient outlet for the passion of love. This was afforded only by that heavenly love which is the love of man for the unseen realities of the spiritual world. The full treatment which this latter subject receives in English poetry testifies to the strong hold which the teachings of Platonism had upon religious experience in the sixteenth and seventeenth centuries. Platonism afforded not only the philosophic basis for the object of this passion, but it also acted as a corrective tendency in checking the influence of an alien idea, erotic mysticism.

Heavenly love, understood as a love known in the soul for a spiritual, or as it was then called, heavenly beauty, sprang out of the treatment to which Plato had subjected love in the "Symposium." In English it appears in two separate forms, although in both it con-

sists in gaining a correct idea of the relation
of the beauty known to the senses as compared
with that known by the soul.   The only difference in the two expressions is that the object
of the passion is variously described.

In Spenser's " Hymne of Heavenly Beautie "
occurs the first form of this love.   The heavenly
beauty celebrated in this " Hymne " is the Platonic wisdom, Sapience, as Spenser calls it, the
same high reality with which he had identified
Una.   (1. 186.)   The subject of the love in the
" Hymne " is formally presented as God, who is
described as

> " that Highest farre beyond all telling,
> Fairer then all the rest which there appeare,
> Though all their beauties joynd together were :
> How then can mortall tongue hope to expresse,
> The image of such endlesse perfectnesse ? "
>
> (ll. 104–108.)

Yet the real subject is the praise of Sapience,
to which somewhat more than one-third of the
" Hymne " is devoted.   A description of her
transcendent beauty and her power to fill the
soul of the beholder with true insight into the
relative beauty of this world of sense and that
of spirit is the climax of the poem.   Among all
the attributes of God mentioned, His truth,

His love, His grace, His mercy, His might,
His judgment (ll. 113–115), the greatest is
Sapience, who is described as sitting in the
very bosom of the Almighty. (l. 187.) The
fairness of her face, he says, none can tell ;
no painter or poet can adequately describe
her ; his own powers are so weak that he
can only admire, not presuming to picture
her. (ll. 207–241.) So completely, however,
does she occupy the field of spiritual vision
in the happy mortals that behold her, that

" Ne from thenceforth doth any fleshly sense,
   Or idle thought of earthly things remaine,
   But all that earst seemd sweet, seemes now offense,
   And all that pleased earst, now seemes to paine,
   Their joy, their comfort, their desire, their gaine,
   Is fixed all on that which now they see,
   All other sights but fayned shadowes bee.

" And that faire lampe, which useth to enflame
   The hearts of men with selfe consuming fyre,
   Thenceforth seemes fowle, and full of sinfull blame;
   And all that pompe, to which proud minds aspyre
   By name of honor, and so much desyre,
   Seemes to them basenesse, and all riches drosse,
   And all mirth sadnesse, and all lucre losse.

" So full their eyes are of that glorious sight,
   And senses fraught with such satietie,
   That in nought else on earth they can delight,

But in th' aspect of that felicitie,
Which they have written in their inward ey;
On which they feed, and in their fastened mynd
All happie joy and full contentment fynd."

(ll. 270–290.)

According to Spenser, then, heavenly love is
the love felt in the soul when the sight of wisdom in her beauty dawns upon the inner vision.
It is a love gained through speculation; and
though the object is conceived of as yonder in
heaven, it is still the beauty which is seen here
in the mind. (l. 17.) Instead of the poetical device of the Mount of Heavenly Contemplation
used in the " Faerie Queene " to signify the refinement of the spiritual vision necessary to the
sight of this heavenly wisdom, Spenser has been
able to explain in detail the way along which
the soul must travel to gain its goal. It is
the dialectic of the " Symposium " (211), the
progress through ever ascending gradations of
beauty up to the first absolute beauty changed
only in the externals as required by the
Christian conception of the heavenly hie-
rarchy. But throughout the long series of
upward stages through which his mind passes,
one may feel the quickening of his spirit at
the thought of the highest beauty, in which

lies the unity of the poem.   In the contemplation of this heavenly beauty the poem begins and ends.

> " Rapt with the rage of mine own ravisht thought,
> Through contemplation of those goodly sights,
> And glorious images in heaven wrought,
> Whose wondrous beauty breathing sweet delights,
> Do kindle love in high conceipted sprights :
> I faine to tell the things that I behold,
> But feele my wits to faile, and tongue to fold."
>
> (ll. 4–10.)

> " And looke at last up to that soveraine light,
> From whose pure beams al perfect beauty springs,
> That kindleth love in every godly spright,
> Even the love of God, which loathing brings
> Of this vile world, and these gay seeming things;
> With whose sweete pleasures being so possest,
> Thy straying thoughts henceforth for ever rest."
>
> (ll. 298–304.)

The second form which the doctrine of heavenly love assumed in English is found in William Drummond's "Song II — It autumn was, and on our hemisphere." The conception of heavenly beauty is not the ethical notion of Spenser's "Hymne," but a less stimulating idea of the beauty of an intelligible world of which this world is but a copy. The attraction in this idea lay in its appeal to Drummond's

peculiar imagination, delighting, as it did, in
the sight of vastness. The poem is an exhortation to the lover, who is Drummond himself,
to cease his mourning for his dead love, and to
raise his mind to a love of heaven and of the
beauty of God there to be seen. The two ideas
which Platonism contributed are the notion of
an intelligible world above this world of sense,
and of an absolute beauty of which all beauty
on earth is but a shadow.

The conception of a world above this world
was suggested by Plato in his "Phædo" and
explained by Plotinus in his Enneads (VI.
vii. 12) as a pure intelligible world. "For
since," says Plotinus, "we say that this All
[the universe] is framed after the Yonder, as
after a pattern, the All must first exist yonder
as a living entity, an animal; and since its idea
is complete, everything must exist yonder.
Heaven, therefore, must exist there as an animal,
not without what here we call its stars, and this
is the idea of heaven. Yonder, too, of course,
must be the Earth, not bare, but far more
richly furnished with life ; in it are all creatures that move on dry land and plants rooted
in life. Sea, too, is yonder, and all water ebb·

ing and flowing in abiding life; and all creatures
that inhabit the water, and all the tribes of the
air are part of the all yonder, and all aerial
beings, for the same reason as Air itself." In
the "Phædo" (110–111), Plato lends color to
his account by calling attention to the fairness
of the place and to the pleasantness of life there.
Drummond has seized upon this idea of an immaterial world where all is fair and happy, and
interprets it as the heaven whither the young
woman who has died is urging him to direct
his love.   Thus in her addresses to Drummond
she speaks of the character of the world where
she lives.

" Above this vast and admirable frame,
    This temple visible, which World we name,

       *   *   *   *   *

There is a world, a world of perfect bliss,
Pure, immaterial, bright, . . .

       *   *   *   *   *

A world, where all is found, that here is found,
But further discrepant than heaven and ground.
It hath an earth, as hath this world of yours,
With creatures peopled, stor'd with trees and flow'rs;
It hath a sea, . . .
It hath pure fire, it hath delicious air,
Moon, sun, and stars, heavens wonderfully fair :

But there flowr's do not fade, trees grow not old,
The creatures do not die through heat nor cold."

(ll. 111–136.)

It is to this world that she urges him to raise
his mind, for all that earth has to offer is a vain
shadow.

" But thou who vulgar footsteps dost not trace,
  Learn to raise up thy mind unto this place,
  And what earth-creeping mortals most affect,
  If not at all to scorn, yet to neglect :
  O chase not shadows vain, which when obtain'd,
  Were better lost, than with such travail gain'd."

(ll. 181–186.)

These shadows are worldly honor and fame.

At this point the poem naturally passes on
to develop the second suggestion found in Platonism, that the beauty of earth is but a
shadow or reflexion of the absolute beauty.
As was common in that time, this absolute
beauty is identified with God. Accordingly,
the young woman appeals to Drummond to
trust in God's beauty, which alone can fill the
soul with bliss. If the power of earthly beauty
— the glance of an eye — can make him leave
all else, what, she asks, must be the love kindled by the " only Fair " ; for though the

wonders of earth, of sea, and heaven are beautiful, they are but shadows of Him.

" O leave that love which reachest but to dust,
   And in that love eternal only trust,
   And beauty, which, when once it is possest,
   Can only fill the soul, and make it blest.
   Pale envy, jealous emulations, fears,
   Sighs, plaints, remorse, here have no place, nor tears;
   False joys, vain hopes, here be not, hate nor wrath;
   What ends all love, here most augments it, death.
   If such force had the dim glance of an eye,
   Which some few days thereafter was to die,
   That it could make thee leave all other things,
   And like the taper-fly there burn thy wings;

     *   *   *   *   *

   If once thou on that only Fair couldst gaze,
   What flames of love would he within thee raise !

     *   *   *   *   *

" Those golden letters which so brightly shine
   In heaven's great volume gorgeously divine;
   The wonders all in sea, in earth, in air,
   Be but dark pictures of that sovereign Fair;
   Be tongues, which still thus cry unto your ear,
   (Could ye amidst world's cataracts them hear,)
   From fading things, fond wights, lift your desire,
   And in our beauty, his, us made, admire:
   If we seem fair, O think how fair is he
   Of whose fair fairness shadows, steps, we be.
   No shadow can compare it with the face,
   No step with that dear foot which did it trace."

                    (ll. 197–234.)

This "Song," then, though drawing on a different phase of Platonism — its more philosophic and fanciful side,[1] not its deep ethical truth — follows the same order of thought as Spenser's "Hymne," and like that presents heavenly love as a love known in the soul and growing out of a correct notion of the relative values of the visible beauty of the senses and the invisible beauty of mind.

In Drummond heavenly love is a progression out of the romantic love of woman. It is not explicitly so stated in the "Song," but in a sonnet, the subject of which refers to the young woman of the longer poem, he writes :

[1] Besides paraphrasing "Phædo," 110-111 in ll. 111-136, Drummond repeats the argument given in that dialogue to prove the probable existence of such a world. Cf. ll. 141-170 with "Phædo," 109. — "But we who live in these hollows [of earth] are deceived into the notion that we are dwelling on the surface of the earth ; which is just as if a creature who was at the bottom of the sea were to fancy that he was on the surface of the water and that the sea was the heaven through which he saw the sun and the other stars, he having never come to the surface by reason of his feebleness and sluggishness, and having never lifted up his head and seen, nor ever heard from one who had seen, how much purer and fairer the world above is than his own . . . [But] if any man could arrive at the exterior limit [of the atmosphere], or take the wings of a bird and come to the top, then like a fish who puts his head out of water and sees this world, he would see a world beyond."

"Sith it hath pleas'd that First and only **Fair**
To take that beauty to himself again,
Which in this world of sense not to remain,
But to amaze, was sent, and home repair;
The love which to that beauty I did bear
(Made pure of mortal spots which did it stain,
And endless, which even death cannot impair),
I place on Him who will it not disdain."

                                    (Poems, Second Pt. S. xiii.)

This is a note heard in other poets where
heavenly love is described as naturally growing out of earthly love when the right idea of
the nature of the object of that lower passion
has been learned.   Thus in Milton it is taught
that the love of woman must not be passion,
but must be a scale by which the mind may
mount to the heavenly world.   The passion
which Adam feels for the loveliness that
hedges the presence of Eve —

"when I approach
Her loveliness, so absolute she seems
And in herself complete, so well to know
Her own, that what she wills to do or say
Seems wisest, virtuousest, discreetest, best:
                *   *   *   *   *
                    and, to consummate all,
Greatness of mind and nobleness their seat
Build in her loveliest, and create an awe
About her, as a guard angelic placed —"

                                    (VIII. 516–559.)

is described by Raphael "with contracted
brow" as merely transported touch, in reality
the same feeling shared by the beasts of the
field. (VIII. 582.) Raphael, accordingly,
directs Adam to love only the rational in Eve's
nature, for true love has his seat in the reason.

> "What higher in her society thou find'st
>   Attractive, human, rational, love still:
>   In loving thou dost well, in passion not,
>   Wherein true Love consists not. Love refines
>   The thoughts, and heart enlarges — hath his seat
>   In Reason, and is judicious, is the scale
>   By which to Heavenly Love thou may'st ascend,
>   Not sunk in carnal pleasure."
>   (VIII. 586–594.)

In Phineas Fletcher's sixth "Piscatorie Eclogue," where there is a long discussion on the
nature of love, human love is shown to be a
love merely of the passing charms of woman:
of her form, which will decay; of her voice,
which is but empty wind; and of her color,
which can move only the sense. (Stz. 20–22.)
No attempt is made to describe the nature of
the higher love, but a simple exhortation to
raise this love of woman to a love of the "God
of fishers" closes the account.

" Then let thy love mount from these baser things,
   And to the Highest Love and worth aspire :
   Love's born of fire, fitted with mounting wings;
   That at his highest he might winde him higher;
   Base love, that to base earth so basely clings!

               *   *   *   *   *

" Raise then thy prostrate love with tow'ring thought ;
   And clog it not in chains and prison here :
   The God of fishers, deare thy love hath bought :
   Most deare He loves ; for shame, love thou as deare."
                                    (Stz. 24, 25.)

Heavenly love, then, whether springing from
the desire within the soul to see wisdom in her
beauty, or from a desire to raise the mind from
a love of earth to the intelligible world, or
from the desire to find a worthy object in the
love of the rational in woman, when freed
from all the grossness of physical passion, is
a contemplative love of a less perishing beauty
than can be found on earth.   And just as the
transition was easy from the love which God
himself knows to the soul's love of God, so was
the change from the love of soul for a higher
reality than earthly beauty to the immortal
love of God for the soul.   Thus in Sidney's
sonnet the subtle change is effected.

" Leave me, O Love, which reachest but to dust,
   And thou my mind aspire to higher things:

Grow rich in that which never taketh rust:
Whatever fades, but fading pleasure brings.
Draw in thy beames, and humble all thy might,
To that sweet yoke, where lasting freedomes be:
Which breakes the clowdes and opens forth the light,
That doth both shine and give us sight to see.
O take fast hold, let that light be thy guide,
In this small course which birth drawes out to death,
And thinke how evill becommeth him to slide,
Who seeketh heav'n, and comes of heav'nly breath.
  Then farewell world, thy uttermost I see,
  Eternall Love maintaine thy life in me."

                                     (S. cx.)

The appeal which Platonism made to the
English poets in its doctrine of a heavenly love
was through its power to stir the minds with
a deep sense of that beauty which God was
understood to possess. The application of the
principle of beauty to God resulted in a note
of joy and in an exaltation of soul in the religious mind, which, after forsaking the beauty
of this world of sense, could enjoy the great
principle of beauty in the beatific vision of
God. Such a strain of joy may be heard in
Drummond, in John Norris, and even in the
quiet lyrics of George Herbert.

The sight of God in His absolute beauty is
considered by these poets as the end of the

soul's endeavor. According to John Norris
God is the divine excellence,

> " Which pleases either *mind* or *sense*,
> Tho' thee by different names we call!
> Search Nature through, there still wilt be
> The *Sum* of all that's good in her *Variety*."

He thus exhorts the soul to rise to a sight of
Him.

> " But do not thou, my Soul, fixt here remain,
> All streams of Beauty here below
> Do from that immense Ocean flow,
> And thither they should lead *again*.
> Trace then these Streams, till thou shalt be
> At length *o'erwhelm'd* in Beauty's *boundless Sea*."
>
> ("Beauty," stz. 4, 10.)

According to Drummond, the one "choicest
bliss" of life is the possession of God's beauty
as a burning passion within the soul. In "An
Hymn of True Happiness" he teaches that supreme felicity does not consist in the enjoyment
of earth's treasures, of sensuous beauty, or of
other sensual delights, and not even in knowledge and fame.

> " No, but blest life is this,
> With chaste and pure desire,
> To turn unto the loadstar of all bliss,
> On God the mind to rest,

Burnt up with sacred fire,
Possessing him, to be by him possesst."

(ll. 61-66.)

" A love which, while it burns
   The soul with fairest beams,
   In that uncreated sun the soul it turns,
   And makes such beauty prove,
   That, if sense saw her gleams,
   All lookers-on would pine and die for love."

(ll. 97-102.)

The essential nature of this beatific vision is described either as a sense of eternal rest or of eternal joy. In Norris's "Prospect," the soul is preparing for the great change that will come when it is free from the body; and its greatest change is described as a sight of "the only Fair."

" Now for the greatest Change prepare,
   To see the only Great, the only Fair,
   Vail now thy feeble eyes, gaze and be blest;
   Here all thy Turns and Revolutions cease,
   Here's all Serenity and Peace :
   Thou'rt to the *Center* come, the native seat of *rest.*
   Here's now no further change nor need there be;
       When *One* shall be *Variety.*"

(Stz. 5.)

In Drummond's " Teares on the Death of Mœliades" the joy of the departed soul is repeatedly emphasized as a rest in the enjoy-

ment of God's beauty. Thus, in closing, the
dead is addressed:

" Rest, blessed spright, rest satiate with the sight
  Of him whose beams doth dazzle and delight,
  Life of all lives, cause of each other cause,
  The sphere and centre where the mind doth pause;
  Narcissus of himself, himself the well,
  Lover, and beauty, that doth all excel.
  Rest, happy ghost, and wonder in that glass
  Where seen is all that shall be, is, or was,
  While shall be, is, or was do pass away,
  And nought remain but an eternal day:
        For ever rest."
                              (ll. 179–188.)

The note of joy in the beatific vision is heard
in Drummond and Norris. In Drummond
earthly love is a care, a war within our nature;
but love

" Among those sprights above
  Which see their Maker's face,
  It a contentment is, a quiet peace,
  A pleasure void of grief, a constant rest,
  Eternal joy which nothing can molest."
                    (" Urania," Madrigal 2.)

And again :

" O blest abode! O happy dwelling-place
  Where visibly th' Invisible doth reign!
  Blest people, who do see true beauty's face,
  With whose dark shadows he but earth doth deign,

All joy is but annoy, all concord strife,
Match'd with your endlesse bliss and happy life."

("Urania," S. v.)

In Norris's "Seraphick Love" a more violent
strain is detected. He has forsaken the beauty
of earth because he has seen a fairer beauty in
contemplation, and to this source of all good and
beauty he thus addresses the close of his poem.

"To thee, thou *only Fair*, my Soul aspires
With *Holy Breathings, languishing* Desires
To thee *m' inamour'd*, panting Heart does move,
By Efforts of *Ecstatic* Love.
How do thy glorious streams of Light
Refresh my intellectual sight!
Tho broken, and strain'd through a Skreen
Of envious Flesh that stands between!
When shall m' imprison'd Soul be free,
That she thy Native Uncorrected Light may see,
And gaze upon thy *Beatifick* Face to all Eternity?"

(Stz. 4.)

The violence of passion in these poets is
absent in George Herbert, and even the
presence of the beatific vision, as a conscious
experience of the soul known after the long
travail of its search for beauty, is not in the
least discernible. Still, the conviction that
there is a higher beauty than that seen on
earth, and that in truth lies this beauty, is

felt beneath the mildness of Herbert's devotion.   In two sonnets, which he sent to
his mother in 1608, he laments the decay of
any true love for God among the poets, and
contrasts the beauty of God with the beauties
of the amorists.   To him the beauty of God
lies in the discovery.

"Such poor invention burns in their [the amorists'] low
        minde,
  Whose fire is wild, and doth not upward go
  To praise, and on Thee, Lord, some ink bestow.
  Open the bones, and you shall nothing finde
  In the best face but filth ; when, Lord, in Thee
  The beauty lies in the discoverie."

                                            (S. i.)

He is, accordingly, content to sing the praises
of God.

"Let foolish lovers, if they will love dung,
  With canvas, not with arras, clothe their shame ;
  Let Follie speak in her own native tongue :
  True Beautie dwells on high ; ours in a flame
  But borrow'd thence to light us thither ;
  Beautie and beauteous words should go together."

                        (" The Forerunners," ll. 25–30.)

So intimately has this notion of the spiritual
nature of true beauty blended with the simple
experience of his devotional life that he can
ask

> " Is there in truth no beautie ?
> Is all good structure in a winding-stair?
> May no lines passe, except they do their dutie
>   Not to a true, but painted chair ?
>
>   *   *   *   *   *
>
> Must purling streams refresh a lover's loves ?
> Must all be vail'd while he that reades divines,
>   Catching the sense at two removes ?"[1]

As for himself, he says :

> " I envie no man's nightingale or spring ;
> Nor let them punish me with loss of rhyme,
> Who plainly say, My God, my King."

("Jordan.")

In that truth he found his beauty.

Platonism, then, came as a direct appeal to the religious mind of the sixteenth and seventeenth centuries which was so constituted that the element of philosophic revery was blended most naturally with a strain of pure devotional love. Although the ultimate postulates of that philosophy were intellectual principles, they were such as could be grasped by the soul only in its deep passion of love for spirit-

---

[1] This idea of catching the truth of a thing at two removes and the reference to a true and painted chair are reminiscences of Plato's discussion of imitative art, and his figure of the three beds. (" Republic " X, 597–599.)

ual beauty.   The condemnation which Baxter
passes upon other philosophies could not be
brought with truth against Platonism. "In
short," he says, "I am an enemy of their
philosophy that vilify sense. . . .   The Scripture that saith of God that He is life and light,
saith also that He is love, and love is complacence, and complacence is joy ; and to say
God is infinite, essential love and joy is a better
notion than with Cartesians and Cocceians to
say that God and angels and spirits are but a
thought or an idea.   What is Heaven to us
if there be no love and joy?"[1]   This desire of
life and love, along its upper levels of thought,
was satisfied by Platonism ; it enabled the poets
to forecast the life of the soul in heaven, and
of its anticipation on earth as a love of beauty.

There was a strong tendency, however,
throughout this period of religious poetry,
toward a phase of devotional love which may
be called erotic mysticism, or that love for
Christ which is characterized less by admiration and more by tenderness and mere delight
in the pure sensuous experience of love.   Con-

[1] "Puritan and Anglican Studies," Edward Dowden, pp.
29–30.

templation of Christ's divine nature as essential beauty is totally absent from this passion. Christ as the object of this love is conceived only as the perfection of physical beauty; and the response within the soul of the lover is that of mere sensuous delight either in the sight of his personal beauties or in the realization of the union with him. This strain of religious devotion is heard in Herbert, in Vaughan, and Crashaw. In Herbert, who confessed that he entered the service of the church in order to be like Christ, "by making humility lovely," — a confession which breathes pure emotion,— there was joined so sensuous a strain that "he seems to rejoice in the thoughts of that word Jesus, and say, that the adding these words, my Master, to it, and often repetition of them, seemed to perfume his mind, and leave an oriental fragrancy in his very breath." [1] The spectacle of the crucified Saviour of man was especially influential in keeping this strain of mystical devotion alive ; and the minds of these poets are continually dwelling upon the beauty of his mangled hands and feet. In a nature so eminently intellectual as John

[1] Walton, "Life of Herbert," pp. 386, 396.

Donne's, this strain of feeling is still present, and in his explanation of the grounds for such a love is found an excellent account of its varying phases. In one of his sermons he says :

" I love my Saviour, as he is *the Lord*, he that studies my salvation : and as *Christ*, made a person able to work my salvation ; but when I see him in the third notion, *Jesus*, accomplishing my salvation, by an actual death, I see those hands stretched out, that stretched out the heavens, and those feet racked, to which they that racked them are footstools : I hear him, from whom his nearest friends fled, pray for his enemies, and him, whom his Father forsook, not forsake his brethren : I see him that clothes this body with his creatures, or else it would wither, and clothes this soul with his righteousness, or else it would perish, hang naked upon the cross ; . . . when I conceit, when I contemplate my Saviour thus, I love the *Lord*, and there is reverent adoration in that love, I love *Christ*, and there is a mysterious adoration in that love, but I love *Jesus*, and there is a tender compassion in that love. . . ." (Works, II. 181.)

Whenever Platonism enters into this tender passion it always elevates the emotion into a higher region, where the more intellectual or spiritual nature of Christ or God is the object of contemplation ; and it does this by affording the poets a conception of the object of the soul's highest love, as a philosophical principle, whether of beauty, of good, or of true being.

The first way by which this elevation of a purely sensuous passion into a higher region was effected was through the Platonic conception of the "idea."   Plato had taught that in love the mind should pass from a sight of the objects of beauty through ever widening circles of abstraction to the contemplation of absolute beauty in its idea.   This can be known only by the soul, and is the only real beauty.   Spenser's "Hymne of Heavenly Love" is the best example of the application of this idea to the love of Christ.   In this poem he sings the praise of Christ as the God of Love.   He finds the chief manifestation of Christ's love in his sacrifice.   At first he treats this as a spectacle to move the eye.   He dwells upon the mangling of Christ's body (ll. 241–247), and exhorts the beholder to

> "bleede in every vaine,
> At sight of his most sacred heavenly corse."
>
> (ll. 251–252.)

But later, instead of calling upon the beholder to lift up his "heavie clouded eye" to behold such a manifestation of mercy (ll. 226–227), he directs him to lift up his *mind* and *meditate* upon the author of his salvation (l. 258). Christ's love then will burn all earthly desire away by the power of

> "that celestiall beauties blaze,"
>
> (l. 280.)

whose glory dazes the eye but illumines the spirit.   And then, when this final stage of refinement is past, the ravished soul of the beholder shall have a sight not of

> "his most sacred heavenly corse"
>
> (l. 252.)

but of the very idea of his pure glory.

> "Then shall thy ravisht soule inspired bee
>   With heavenly thoughts, farre above humane skill,
>   And thy bright radiant eyes shall plainely see
>   Th' Idee of his pure glorie present still,
>   Before thy face, that all thy spirits shall fill
>   With sweet enragement of celestiall love,
>   Kindled through sight of those faire things above."
>
> (ll. 284–290.)

The "Hymne," which celebrates the life of
Christ on earth as a man among men, closes, as
it had begun, with the mind in the presence of
heavenly beauty.

In Phineas Fletcher the term "idea" is not
used, but the habit of thought is identical with
that of Spenser's.   Christ is to be seen by the
soul, not in his bodily form, but in his "first
beautie" and "true majestie."   In the passage
where these expressions occur Fletcher is showing the manner of the love we should bestow
upon Christ for that which he has shown to us.
He says that the only adequate return is to give
back to Christ the love he has given to us.
He then prays that Christ will inflame man
with his glorious ray in order that he may rise
above a love of earthly things into heaven.

"So we beholding with immortall eye
    The glorious picture of Thy heav'nly face,
    In His first beautie and true Majestie,
    May shake from our dull souls these fetters base;
    And mounting up to that bright crystal sphere,
    Whence Thou strik'st all the world with shudd'ring fear,
    May not be held by earth, nor hold vile earth so deare."
                    (" The Purple Island," VI. 75.)

In Crashaw's " In the Glorious Epiphanie of
Our Lord God," the elevation of the subject from

a sensuous image into an object of pure contemplation is effected by conceiving Christ's nature as that of true being according to the Platonic notion.   The first image brought before the mind is that of the Christ child's face.

> " Bright Babe! Whose awfull beautyes make
> The morn incurr a sweet mistake ;
> For Whom the officious Heavns devise
> To disinheritt the sun's rise:
> Delicately to displace
> The day, and plant it fairer in Thy face."
>
> (ll. 1–5.)

Soon, however, under this image of the face appears the hidden conception of Christ as true being unchanging and everywhere present. For Christ is addressed as

> " All-circling point! all-centring sphear!
> The World's one, round, aeternall year:
> Whose full and all-unwrinkled face
> Nor sinks nor swells with time or place;
> But every where and every while
> Is one consistent, solid smile."
>
> (ll. 26– 31.)

The poem, then, which had begun with a recognition of the beauty of the Babe's eyes in whose beauty the East had come to seek itself, ends in a desire not to know what may be seen with

the eyes, but to press on, upward to a purely
intellectual object, — Christ in heaven.

> " Thus we, who when with all the noble powres
> That (at Thy cost) are call'd not vainly, ours:
> We vow to make brave way
> Upwards, and presse on for the pure intelligentiall
> prey."
>
> (ll. 220–223.)

In those passages in Henry More, where the
mystic union of the soul with Christ or God is
symbolized as a sensuous experience, the elevating power of Platonism is noticeable in the
progression of the poet's mind out of this lower
plane into a higher region of pure thought.
Thus in " Psychathanasia " the advance is made
from a treatment of the communion, which
the blest have with Christ in their partaking
His body and blood, to a contemplation of the
beauty of God.   In this union, which is shared
by those

> " whose souls *deiform* summitie
> Is waken'd in this life, and so to God
> Are nearly joynd in a firm Unitie,"
>
> (III. i. 30.)

the true believers grow incorporate with Christ.

> " Christ is the sunne that by his chearing might
> Awakes our higher rayes to joyn with his pure light.

" And when he hath that life elicited,
He gives his own dear body and his bloud
To drink and eat.   Thus dayly we are fed
Unto eternall life.   Thus do we bud,
True heavenly plants, suck in our lasting food
From the first spring of life, incorporate
Into the higher world (as erst I show'd
Our lower rayes the soul to subjugate
To this low world) we fearlesse sit above all fate,

" Safely that kingdomes glory contemplate,
O'erflow with joy by a full sympathie
With that worlds spright, and blesse our own estate
Praising the fount of all felicitie,
The lovely light of the blest Deitie.
Vain mortals think on this, and raise your mind
Above the bodies life; strike through the skie
With piercing throbs and sighs, that you may find
His face.   Base fleshly fumes your drowsie eyes thus
          blind."

                                        (III. i. 31–33.)

In Giles Fletcher's "Christ's Triumph after
Death" the most elaborate attempt is made to
convey the idea of the blessedness of the union
of the soul with God through the pleasure of
mere sense and at the same time to show how
the object with which the soul is joined is in
every respect a super-sensible entity.   At first
the blessedness of the soul's life in heaven is
presented both as a pleasurable enjoyment of

the sense of sight, of hearing, and even that of
smell, and as a more spiritual pleasure in the
exercise of the faculties of understanding and
will. Speaking of the joy of those souls that
ever hold

" Their eyes on Him, whose graces manifold
The more they doe behold, the more they would behold,"

Fletcher says :

" Their sight drinkes lovely fires in at their eyes,
Their braine sweet incense with fine breath accloyes,
That on God's sweating altar burning lies ;
Their hungrie eares feede on the heav'nly noyse,
That angels sing, to tell their untould joyes;
Their understanding, naked truth ; their wills
The all, and selfe-sufficient Goodnesse, fills :
That nothing here is wanting, but the want of ills."
(Stz. 34.)

Here the progression in the scale of pleasures is
from those of the senses to those of the mind.

But Fletcher presents this union as even a
more intimate experience of the soul. His is
the most elaborate attempt in English poetry
to describe the nature of the participation of
the soul in the beauty of the ultimate reality,
according to the Platonic notion of the participation of an object in its idea. After three
stanzas descriptive of the state of absolute

freedom from cares of life which reigns in heaven
(stz. 35–37), Fletcher passes on to a description of God — the " Idea Beatificall," as he
names Him — in accordance with the Platonic
notion of the highest principle, The One :

> " In midst of this citie cælestiall,
>   Whear the Eternall Temple should have rose,
>   Light'ned the Idea Beatificall :
>   End, and beginning of each thing that growes;
>   Whose selfe no end, nor yet beginning knowes;
>   That hath no eyes to see, nor ears to heare;
>   Yet sees, and heares, and is all-eye, all-eare;
>   That nowhear is contain'd, and yet is every whear :

> " Changer of all things, yet immutable ;
>   Before and after all, the first and last;
>   That, mooving all, is yet immoveable ;
>   Great without quantitie : in Whose forecast
>   Things past are present, things to come are past;
>   Swift without motion ; to Whose open eye
>   The hearts of wicked men unbrested lie ;
>   At once absent and present to them, farre, and nigh."
>   (Stz. 39–40.)

He then goes on to explain what the Idea is not.
It is nothing that can be known by sense.   It
is no flaming lustre, no harmony of sounds, no
ambrosial feast for the appetite, no odor, no soft
embrace, nor any sensual pleasure.   And yet
within the soul of the beholder it is known

as an inward feast, a harmony, a light, a sound,
a sweet perfume, and entire embrace. Thus
he writes :

" It is no flaming lustre, made of light;
  No sweet concent, as well-tim'd harmonie;
  Ambrosia, for to feast the appetite,
  Or flowrie odour, mixt with spicerie ;
  No soft embrace, or pleasure bodily ;
  And yet it is a kinde of inward feast,
  A harmony, that sounds within the brest,
  An odour, light, embrace, in which the soule doth rest.

" A heav'nly feast, no hunger can consume ;
  A light unseene, yet shines in every place ;
  A sound, no time can steale ; a sweet perfume
  No winds can scatter ; an intire embrace
  That no satietie can ere unlace."
                                        (Stz. 41–42.)

Such was the powerful hold of the doctrines
of Platonism upon the minds of these religious poets.   Strong as were the forces leading
them into a degenerate form of Christian love,
these were overcome by the one fundamental
conception of Platonism that the highest love
the soul can know is the love of a purely intellectual principle of beauty and goodness ; and
that this love is one in which passion and
reason are wedded into the one supreme

desire of the seeker after wisdom and beauty.
Such a conception saved a large body of
English poetry from degenerating into that
form of erotic mysticism which Crashaw's later
poems reveal; and in which there is no elevation of the mind away from the lower range of
sense enjoyment, but only an introversion of the
physical life into the intimacies of spiritual
experience.

II. EARTHLY LOVE

The influence of Platonism upon the love
poetry of the sixteenth and seventeenth centuries in England is felt in two distinct forms.
In the first place, the teachings of that philosophy were used to explain and dignify the
conception of love as a passion having its
source in a desire for the enjoyment of beauty;
and in the second place, the emphasis laid by
Platonism upon the function of the soul as opposed to the senses resulted in a tendency to
treat love as a purely spiritual passion devoid
of all sensuous pleasure. In the first phase the
teachings of Platonic theory were made to ren-
der service according to the conventional love
theory known as Petrarchism; and in its second

phase Platonism contributed its share in keeping alive the so-called metaphysical mood of the seventeenth-century lyric.

According to the conventional method of Petrarchism, the object of the poet's love was always a lady of great beauty and spotless virtue, and of a correspondingly great cruelty. Hence the subjects of the Petrarchian love poem were either the praise of the mistress's beauty or an account of the torment of soul caused by her heartless indifference. By applying the doctrines of Platonism to this conventional manner, a way was found to explain upon a seemingly philosophic basis the power of the lover's passion and of beauty as its exciting cause. The best example in English of this application of Platonic theory is Spenser's two hymns, — "An Hymne in Honour of Love" and "An Hymne in Honour of Beautie."

The professed aim of Spenser in these hymns differs in no wise from the purpose of the Petrarchian lover. Both are written to ease the torments of an unrequited passion. In the "Hymne in Honour of Love" he addresses love in his invocation :

> " Love, that long since hast to thy mighty powre,
> Perforce subdude my poore captived hart,
> And raging now therein with restlesse stowre,
> Doest tyrannize in everie weaker part;
> Faine would I seeke to ease my bitter smart,
> By any service I might do to thee,
> Or ought that else might to thee pleasing bee."
>
> (ll. 4–10.)

In his closing stanzas he expresses the wish of coming at last to the object of his desire. (ll. 298–300.) In the "Hymne in Honour of Beautie," he openly confesses a desire that through his hymn

> " It may so please that she at length will streame
> Some deaw of grace, into my withered hart,
> After long sorrow and consuming smart."
>
> (ll. 29–31.)

The only respect in which these hymns differ from the mass of love poetry of their time is in the method by which Spenser treated the common subject of the poetical amorists of the Renaissance. In singing the praises of love and beauty he drew upon the doctrines of Italian Platonism, and by the power of his own genius blended the purely expository and lyrical strains so that at times it is difficult to separate them. The presence of Platonic doc-

trine, however, is felt in the dignified treatment
of the passion of love and of beauty.

In the "Hymne in Honour of Love" love is
described as no merely cruel passion inflicted
by the tyrannical Cupid of the amorist, but as
the manifestation in man of the great informing power which brought the universe out of
chaos and which now maintains it in order and
concord. According to Ficino, the greatest
representative of Italian Platonism during the
Renaissance, one truth established by the speech
of Eryximachus in the "Symposium" is that
love is the creator and preserver of all things.
"Through this," Ficino says in his "Commentarium in Convivium," "fire moves air by shar-
ing its heat ; the air moves the water, the water
moves the earth; and *vice versa* the earth draws
the water to itself; water, the air ; and the air,
the fire. Plants and trees also beget their like
because of a desire of propagating their seed.
Animals, brutes, and men are allured by the
same desire to beget offspring." (III. 2.) And
in summing up his discussion he says, "Therefore all parts of the universe, since they are the
work of one artificer and are members of the
same mechanism like to one another both in

being and in life, are linked together by a certain mutual love, so that love may be rightly
declared the perpetual bond of the universe and
the unmoving support of its parts and the firm
basis of the whole mechanism." (III. 3.) Holding to this conception of love Spenser comes to
a praise of the

> " Great god of might, that reignest in the mynd,
> And all the bodie to thy hest doest frame,"
>
> (ll. 46–47.)

with an explanation of His power as the creating
and sustaining spirit of the universe.   Before
the world was created love moved over the
warring elements of chaos and arranged them
in the order they now obey.

> " Then through the world his way he gan to take,
> The world that was not till he did it make;
> Whose sundrie parts he from them selves did sever,
> The which before had lyen confused ever,

> " The earth, the ayre, the water, and the fyre,
> Then gan to raunge them selves in huge array,
> And with contrary forces to conspyre
> Each against other, by all meanes they may,
> Threatning their owne confusion and decay:
> Ayre hated earth, and water hated fyre,
> Till Love relented their rebellious yre.

" He then them tooke, and tempering goodly well
  Their contrary dislikes with loved meanes,
  Did place them all in order, and compell
  To keepe them selves within their sundrie raines,
  Together linkt with Adamantine chaines."

                                  (ll. 77–92.)

The second subject which was treated in the light of Platonism was that of beauty. In the " Hymne in Honour of Beautie " the topic is treated from three points of view. First, the " Hymne " outlines a general theory of æsthetics to account for the presence of beauty in the universe lying without us (ll. 32–87) ; second, it explains the ground of reason for the beauty to be found in the human body (ll. 88–164) ; and third, it accounts for the exaggerated notion which the lover has of his beloved's physical perfections. (ll. 214–270.)

Spenser's general theory of æsthetics is a blending of two suggestions he found in his study of Platonism. According to Ficino, beauty is a spiritual thing, the splendor of God's light shining in all things. (II. 5; V. 4.) This conception is based upon the idea that the universe is an emanation of God's spirit, and that beauty is the lively grace of the divine light of God shining in matter. (V. 6.)

But according to another view, the universe is conceived as the objective work of an artificer, working according to a pattern. "The work of the creator," says Plato in the "Timæus" (28, 29), "whenever he looks to the unchangeable and fashions the form and the nature of his work after an unchangeable pattern, must necessarily be made fair and perfect. . . . If the world be indeed fair and the artificer good, it is manifest that he must have looked to that which is eternal. . . . for the world is the fairest of creations and he is the best of causes." By blending these ideas Spenser was able to conceive of God as creating the world after a pattern of ideal beauty, which, by virtue of its infusion into matter, is the source of that lively grace which the objects called beautiful possess. At first he presents the view of creation which is more in accordance with the Mosaic account,

> " What time this worlds great workmaister did cast
> To make al things, such as we now behold :
> It seemes that he before his eyes had plast
> A goodly Paterne to whose perfect mould,
> He fashioned them as comely as he could,
> That now so faire and seemely they appeare,
> As nought may be amended any wheare.

" That wondrous Paterne
          *   *   *   *   *
Is perfect Beautie, which all men adore,
Whose face and feature doth so much excell
All mortall sence, that none the same may tell."
(ll. 32–45.)

Spenser now passes on to the theory of the
infusion of beauty in matter, by which its
grossness is refined and quickened, as it were,
into life.

" Thereof as every earthly thing partakes,
   Or more or lesse by influence divine,
   So it more faire accordingly it makes,
   And the grosse matter of this earthly myne,
   Which clotheth it, thereafter doth refyne,
   Doing away the drosse which dims the light
   Of that faire beame, which therein is empight.

" For through infusion of celestiall powre,
   The duller earth it quickneth with delight
   And life-full spirits privily doth powre
   Through all the parts, that to the looker's sight
   They seeme to please.   That is thy soveraine might,
   O *Cyprian* Queene, which flowing from the beame
   Of thy bright starre, then into them doest streame."
(ll. 46–59.)

At this point of his " Hymne " Spenser pauses
to refute the idea that beauty is

" An outward shew of things, that only seeme "
(l. 94.)

His pausing to overthrow such an idea of beauty is quite in the manner of the scientific expositor in the Italian treatises and dialogues written throughout the Renaissance. Ficino, for instance, combats the idea, which he says some hold, that beauty is nothing but the proportion of the various parts of an object with a certain sweetness of color. (V. 3.) In like manner Spenser says it is the idle wit that identifies beauty with proportion and color, both of which pass away.

> " How vainely then doe ydle wits invent,
>   That beautie is nought else, but mixture made
>   Of colours faire, and goodly temp'rament,
>   Of pure complexions, that shall quickly fade
>   And passe away, like to a sommers shade,
>   Or that it is but comely composition
>   Of parts well measurd, with meet disposition."

(ll. 67-73.)

Spenser overthrows this contention by doubting the power of mere color and superficial proportion to stir the soul of man. (ll. 74-87.) He has proved the power of beauty only too well to maintain such a theory. He thus seeks for the source of its power in the soul.

The Platonic theory of beauty teaches that the beauty of the body is a result of the

formative energy of the soul.   According to
Ficino, the soul has descended from heaven and
has framed a body in which to dwell.   Before
its descent it conceives a certain plan for the
forming of a body; and if on earth it finds
material favorable for its work and sufficiently
plastic, its earthly body is very similar to its
celestial one, hence it is beautiful.   (VI. 6.)
In Spenser this conception underlies his account
of the descent of the soul from God to earth.

> " For when the soule, the which derived was
>   At first, out of that great immortall Spright,
>   By whom all live to love, whilome did pas
>   Downe from the top of purest heavens hight,
>   To be embodied here, it then tooke light
>   And lively spirits from that fayrest starre,
>   Which lights the world forth from his firie carre.

> " Which powre retayning still or more or lesse,
>   When she in fleshly seede is eft enraced,
>   Through every part she doth the same impresse,
>   According as the heavens have her graced,
>   And frames her house, in which she will be placed,
>   Fit for her selfe, adorning it with spoyle
>   Of th' heavenly riches, which she robd erewhyle.

> *   *   *   *   *

> " So every spirit, as it is most pure,
>   And hath in it the more of heavenly light,
>   So it the fairer bodie doth procure

> To habit in, and it more fairely dight
> With chearefull grace and amiable sight.
> For of the soule the bodie forme doth take:
> For soul is forme, and doth the bodie make."
>
> (ll. 109–136.)

The obvious objection which one might make to this theory, that it does not cover the whole ground inasmuch as it could never account for the fact of the existence of a good soul in any but a beautiful form, was answered by the further explanation that when the matter of which the soul makes its body is unyielding, the soul must content itself with a less beautiful form. (Ficino, VI. 6.) Thus Spenser adds:

> "Yet oft it falles, that many a gentle mynd
> Dwels in deformed tabernacle drownd,
> Either by chaunce, against the course of kynd,
> Or through unaptnesse in the substance sownd,
> Which it assumed of some stubborne grownd,
> That will not yield unto her formes direction,
> But is perform'd with some foule imperfection."
>
> (ll. 144–150.)

After an exhortation to the "faire Dames" to keep their souls unspotted (ll. 165–200), Spenser outlines the true manner of love and in the course of his poem he accounts for that manifestation of power which the beloved's beauty

has over the mind of the lover.   According to
Ficino, true lovers are those whose souls have
departed from heaven under the same astral
influences and who, accordingly, are informed
with the same idea in imitation of which they
frame their earthly bodies. (VI. 6.)   Thus
Spenser writes that love is not a matter of
chance, but a union of souls ordained by
heaven.

" For Love is a celestiall harmonie,
    Of likely harts composd of starres concent,
    Which joyne together in sweet sympathie,
    To work ech others joy and true content,
    Which they have harbourd since their first descent
    Out of their heavenly bowres, where they did see
    And know ech other here belov'd to bee.

" Then wrong it were that any other twaine
    Should in loves gentle band combyned bee,
    But those whom heaven did at first ordaine,
    And made out of one mould the more t' agree :
    For all that like the beautie which they see,
    Streight do not love : for love is not so light,
    As straight to burne at first beholders sight."
                                        (ll. 200–213.)

He then explains the Platonist's views of
love as a passion.   Ficino had stated that the
lover is not satisfied with the mere visual image
of the beloved, but refashions it in accordance

with the idea of the beloved which he has;
for the two souls departing from heaven at the
same time were informed with the same idea.
The lover, then, when he beholds the person of
the beloved, sees a form which has been made
more in conformity with the idea than his own
body has; consequently he loves it, and by
refining the visual image of the beloved from
all the grossness of sense, he beholds in it the
idea of his own soul and that of the beloved;
and in the light of this idea he praises the
beloved's beauty. (VI. 6.) So Spenser:

> " But they which love indeede, looke otherwise,
> With pure regard and spotlesse true intent,
> Drawing out of the object of their eyes,
> A more refyned forme, which they present
> Unto their mind, voide of all blemishment;
> Which it reducing to her first perfection,
> Beholdeth free from fleshes frayle infection."
>
> (ll. 214–220.)

Here there is no distinction of lover and
beloved; but soon Spenser passes on to consider the subject from the lover's standpoint:

> " And then conforming it unto the light,
> Which in it selfe it hath remaining still
> Of that first Sunne, yet sparckling in his sight,
> Thereof he fashions in his higher skill,

An heavenly beautie to his fancies will,
And it embracing in his mind entyre,
The mirrour of his owne thought doth admyre.

"Which seeing now so inly faire to be,
As outward it appeareth to the eye,
And with his spirits proportion to agree,
He thereon fixeth all his fantasie,
And fully setteth his felicitie,
Counting it fairer, then it is indeede,
And yet indeede her fairenesse doth exceede."
                                        (ll. 221-234.)

With a description of the many beauties the
lover sees in the beloved — the thousands of
graces that make delight on her forehead — the
poem ends.   (ll. 235-270.)

The feature in this theory of Platonism which
appealed to Spenser was the high nature of the
beauty seen in comeliness of form, as explained
by its doctrine of æsthetics.   A sense of beauty
as a spiritual quality spreading its divine radiance over the objects of the outward world
envelops the poem in a golden haze of softened
feeling characteristic of Spenser's poetic manner.
The scientific terms of the Platonic theorist melt
away into the gentle flow of his verse.   The
soul being informed with its idea, as Ficino
had put it, has become in his " Hymne in

Honour of Beautie " that "faire lampe" which has "resemblence of that heavenly light" of beauty (ll. 102, 124); or the idea of beauty in the soul is spoken of as

> "the light
> Which in it selfe it hath remaining still;"
>
> (ll. 221-222.)

or, as the lover's "spirits proportion."

In accordance with the same sense of beauty Spenser in the "Hymne in Honour of Love" stops to explain away the cruelty which love seems to show in afflicting him, an innocent sufferer, by calling attention to the fact that such suffering is necessary to try the lover's sincerity in his worship of so high a thing as the beauty of his beloved. Love is not physical desire, but a soaring of the mind to a sight of that high beauty,

> "For love is Lord of truth and loialtie,
>   Lifting himselfe out of the lowly dust,
>   On golden plumes up to the purest skie,
>   Above the reach of loathly sinfull lust,
>
> *   *   *   *   *
>
> "Such is the powre of that sweet passion,
>   That it all sordid basenesse doth expell,
>   And the refyned mynd doth newly fashion
>   Unto a fairer forme which now doth dwell

> In his high thought, that would it selfe excell;
> Which he beholding still with constant sight,
> Admires the mirrour of so heavenly light."
>
> (ll. 179–199.)

And even though the lover may not win the good graces of his lady, he is happy in the sight of her beauty.

> " And though he do not win his wish to end,
> Yet thus farre happie he him selfe doth weene,
> That heavens such happie grace did to him lend,
> No thing on earth so heavenly, to have seene,
> His harts enshrined saint, his heavens queene,
> Fairer then fairest, in his fayning eye,
> Whose sole aspect he counts felicitye."
>
> (ll. 214–220.)

Because of this love of beauty, Spenser was able to find more material in the Renaissance criticism of Platonic æsthetics for his " Hymne in Honour of Beautie " than in the corresponding hymn on love. Besides the conception of the creative power of love, his " Hymne in Honour of Love " draws upon a few suggestions which could dignify the power of the passion. The saying of Diotima to Socrates in the " Symposium," — " Marvel not then at the love which all men have of their offspring ; for that universal love and interest is for the sake

of immortality" (208)—is made to do service
in differentiating the passion of love in men
from that in beasts. By satisfying physical
desire beasts

> "all do live, and moved are
> To multiply the likenesse of their kynd,
> Whilest they seeke onely, without further care,
> To quench the flame, which they in burning fynd:
> But man, that breathes a more immortal mynd,
> Not for lusts sake, but for eternitie,
> Seekes to enlarge his lasting progenie."
>
> (ll. 102–109.)

Further, to add a sense of mystery to the
nativity of the god of love, Spenser refers to
the myth of Penia and Poros, and also in the
manner of the Platonist tries to reconcile two
contrary assertions about the mysterious nature
of love's birth. In Diotima's account of "the
lesser mysteries of love," she says that love is
the offspring of the god Poros or Plenty, and of
Penia or Poverty. ("Symposium," 203.) In
Phædrus's oration on love he began by affirm-
ing that "Love is a mighty god, and wonderful
among gods and men, but especially wonderful
in his birth. For he is the eldest of the gods."
("Symposium," 178.) Agathon, however, differs from his friend Phædrus in saying that love

is the youngest of the gods. ("Symposium,"
195.) This disagreement was a source of per-
plexity to the Platonist of the Renaissance ;
thus Ficino gives a division of his commentary
to a reconciliation of these statements. (V. 10.)
He solves the difficulty by stating that when
the Creator conceived the order of angels, with
whom Ficino identifies the gods of ancient
mythology, the love guiding God was before
the angels, hence is the most ancient of the
gods ; but when the created angelic intelli-
gences turned in their love to the Creator, the
impelling love was the youngest, coming after
the creation of the angels. According to these
notions of the nativity of the god of love,
Spenser opens his "Hymne."

" Great god of might, that reignest in the mynd,
  And all the bodie to thy hest doest frame,
  Victor of gods, subduer of mankynd,
  That doest the Lions and fell Tigers tame,
  Making their cruell rage thy scornefull game,
  And in their roring taking great delight;
  Who can expresse the glorie of thy might?

" Or who alive can perfectly declare,
  The wondrous cradle of thine infancie?
  When thy great mother *Venus* first thee bare,
  Begot of Plentie and of Penurie,

Though elder then thine owne nativitie :
And yet a chyld, renewing still thy yeares ;
And yet the eldest of the heavenly Peares."

(ll. 46-59.)

Spenser's "Hymnes" are the most comprehensive exposition of love in the light of Platonic theory in English. The attempt, however, which he made to place love upon a basis of philosophic fact is imitated in a much less prominent way in other poets. Spenser himself refers to the subject in "Colin Clouts Come Home Againe." In that poem Colin unfolds to Cuddy the high nature of love's perfection. At the court, he says, love is the all-engrossing topic (ll. 778-786); but it is love so shamefully licentious that its "mightie mysteries" are profaned. (l. 790.) Love, however, is a religious thing and should be so conceived. To support this statement Colin explains the creative power of love manifest throughout the wide range of nature (ll. 843-868) and points out that in man it is a love of beauty. (ll. 869-880).

In a few of Jonson's masques there are slight attempts to dignify the subject of love in the manner of Spenser's "Hymnes." In "The Masque of Beauty" love is described as the

creator of the universe, and beauty is mentioned
as that for which the world was created.   In
one of the hymns occurs this stanza :

" When Love at first, did move
  From out of Chaos, brightned
  So was the world, and lightned
  As now.
            1. Echo. As now !
                        2. Echo. As now !
  Yield Night, then to the light,
  As Blackness hath to Beauty :
  Which is but the same duty.
  It was for Beauty that the world was made,
  And where she reigns, Love's lights admit no shade."

In a second song a reference is made to the
mysterious nativity of love.

" So Beauty on the waters stood,
  When Love had sever'd earth from flood !
  So when he parted air from fire,
  He did with concord all inspire !
  And then a motion he them taught,
  That elder than himself was thought.
  Which thought was, yet, the child of earth,
  For Love is elder than his birth."

In " Love's Triumph Through Callipolis " the
same ideas appear.   In this masque, after the
band of sensual lovers has been driven from
the suburbs of the City of Beauty (Callipolis),

and a lustration of the place has followed,
Euclia, or "a fair glory, appears in the heavens,
singing an applausive Song, or Pæan of the
whole."

> "So love emergent out of chaos brought
>   The world to light!
> And gently moving on the waters, wrought
>   All form to sight!
>   Love's appetite
>   Did beauty first excite:
>   And left imprinted in the air
>   These signatures of good and fair,
> Which since have flow'd, flow'd forth upon the sense
> To wonder first, and then to excellence,
> By virtue of divine intelligence!"

In the same masque love is defined in accordance with the myth of Penia and Poros :

> "Love is the right affection of the mind,
>   The noble appetite of what is best:
> Desire of union with the thing design'd,
>   But in fruition of it cannot rest.

> "The father Plenty is, the mother Want,
>   Plenty the beauty which it wanteth draws;
> Want yields itself: affording what is scant:
>   So both affections are the union's cause."

In "Love Freed From Ignorance and Folly"
the sustaining power of love in keeping the

parts of the universe in concord is used to combat the accusation that love is mere cruelty. Love, who is represented as a captive of the Sphynx, thus replies to the charge :

> "Cruel Sphynx, I rather strive
> How to keep the world alive,
> And uphold it; without me,
> All again would chaos be."

In "The Barriers" where Truth and Opinion — a division of the state of knowing according to its degree of certainty common in Plato as knowledge and opinion ("Republic," V. 476–478) — hold a discussion on marriage, an angel declares that

> "Eternal Unity behind her [*i.e.* Truth] shines,
> That fire and water, earth and air combines."

Here under the name of Unity the true nature of love is indicated.

In Drayton's seventh eclogue Batte replies to a charge of cruelty against love which is made by his fellow-shepherd, Borril, with the

> "substancyall ryme
> that to thy teeth sufficiently shall proove
> there is no power to be compard to love."

His argument is that love is the great bond of the universe.

" What is Love but the desire
    of tho thing that fancy pleaseth?
A holy and resistlesse fiere
    weake and strong alike that ceaseth,
    which not heaven hath power to let
Nor wise nature cannot smother,
    whereby Phœbus doth begette
    on the universal mother.
    that the everlasting chaine
    which together al things tied,
    and unmooved them retayne
    and by which they shall abide;
    that concent we cleerely find
    all things doth together drawe,
    and so strong in every kinde
    subjects them to natures law.
    whose hie virtue number teaches
    in which every thing dooth moove,
    from the lowest depth that reaches
    to the height of heaven above."

                        (ll. 165–184.)

A more common appropriation of the teachings of Platonism was made in the love lyrics
— chiefly the sonnet — written in the Petrarchian manner.   Petrarchism was as much a
manner of writing sonnets as it was a method
of making love.   On its stylistic side it was
characterized by the use of antitheses, puns,
and especially of conceits.   In the Platonic
theory of love and beauty a certain amount of

material was offered which could be reworked
into a form suited for the compact brevity of
the sonnet. Sidney, Spenser, and Shakespeare
are the three chief sonnet writers of the last
decade of the sixteenth century in whose
work this phase of Platonism is to be found;
but its presence, though faint, can be felt in
others.

One way in which this theory was applied
is found in the manner in which these poets
speak of the beauty of their beloved. Plato
has stated that wisdom is the most lovely of
all ideas, and that, were there a visible image
of her, she would be transporting. ("Phædrus,"
250.) Sidney seizes upon this suggestion, and
by identifying his Stella with wisdom he can
frame a sonnet ending in a couplet that shall
have the required epigrammatic point. He
writes:

" The wisest scholler of the wight most wise,
  By *Phœbus* doome, with sugred sentence sayes:
  That vertue if it once meete with our eyes,
  Strange flames of love it in our soules would rayse.
    But for that man with paine this truth discries,
    While he each thing in sences ballances wayes,
  And so, nor will nor can behold these skyes,
  Which inward Sunne to heroicke mindes displaies.

Vertue of late with vertuous care to stir
Love of himselfe, takes *Stellas* shape, that hee
To mortal eyes might sweetly shine in her.
It is most true, for since I did her see,
   Vertues great beautie in her face I prove,
   And finde defect; for I doe burne in love."

                                      (xxv.)

Shakespeare is able to praise the beauty of
the subject of his sonnets by identifying him
with the absolute beauty of the Platonic philosophy, and by describing him in accordance
with this notion. Thus he confesses that his
argument is simply the fair, kind, and true, back
of which statement may be inferred the theory
upheld by Platonism that the good, the beautiful, and the true are but different phases of
one reality. His love, he says, cannot be called
idolatry because his songs are directed to this
theme, for only in his friend are these three
themes united into one.

"Let not my love be call'd idolatry,
  Nor my belovéd as an idol show,
  Since all alike my songs and praises be
  To one, of one, still such, and ever so.
  Kind is my love to-day, to-morrow kind,
  Still constant in a wondrous excellence;
  Therefore my verse to constancy confined,
  One thing expressing, leaves out difference.

' Fair, kind, and true ' is all my argument,
' Fair, kind, and true ' varying to other words ;
And in this change is my invention spent,
Three themes in one, which wondrous scope affords.
' Fair, kind, and true,' have often liv'd alone,
Which three, till now, never kept seat in one."

(cv.)

In another sonnet one phase of this argument
is given a detailed treatment, and the poet's
object is to praise the beauty of his friend by
describing its contrast with the beauty of earth,
just as if he were speaking of absolute beauty.
In this sonnet he uses the Platonic phraseology
of the substance and the shadow, by which he
means first, the reality that makes a thing what
it is, the substance, not the matter or stuff of
which it is made ; and second, the reflection of
that reality in the objective world, the shadow
of the substance, not the obscuration of light.[1]
He thus writes of his friend's beauty as if it
were the substance of beauty, beauty absolute,
of which all other beauty is but a reflection.

"What is your substance, whereof are you made,
   That millions of strange shadows on you tend ?
   Since every one hath, every one, one shade,

[1] Poems of Shakespeare.   Ed. George Wyndham, p.
cxxii.

And you, but one, can every shadow lend.
Describe *Adonis*, and the counterfeit
Is poorly imitated after you;
On *Helen's* cheek all art of beauty set,
And you in *Grecian* tires are painted new:
Speak of the spring and foison of the year,
The one doth shadow of your beauty show,
The other as your bounty doth appear;
And you in every blesséd shape we know,
In all external grace you have some part,
But you like none, none you, for constant heart."

(liii.)

Spenser, too, praises his beloved by conceiving her as absolute beauty, of which all other objects are but shadows. In the light of her beauty all the glory of the world appears but a vain show.

" My hungry eyes through greedy covetize,
    still to behold the object of their paine:
    with no contentment can themselves suffize.
    but having pine and having not complaine.
For lacking it they cannot lyfe sustayne,
    and having it they gaze on it the more:
    in their amazement lyke *Narcissus* vaine
    whose eyes him starv'd: so plenty makes me **poore**.
Yet are mine eyes so filled with the store
    of that faire sight, that nothing else they brooke,
    but lothe the things which they did like before,
    and can no more endure on them to looke.
All this worlds glory seemeth vayne to me,
    and all their showes but shadowes saving she."

(**xxxv.**)

In George Daniel the idea of the substance
and shadow again occurs. He says that it is
enough for him if he may behold his mistress's
face, although others may boast of her favors ;
for in contemplating her glories he sees how all
other forms are but empty shadows of her perfection.

> " It is Enough to me,
>   If I her Face may see ;
> Let others boast her Favours, and pretend
>   Huge Interests ; whilst I
>   Adore her Modestie ;
> Which Tongues cannot deprave, nor Swords defend.
>
>   *   *   *   *   *
>
> " But while I bring
>   My verse to Sing
> Her Glories, I am strucke with wonder, more ;
>   And all the Formes I see,
>   But Emptie Shadowes bee,
> Of that Perfection which I adore.
>
> " Be silent then,
>   All Tongues of Men,
> To Celebrate the Sex : for if you fall
>   To other Faces, you
>   Wander, and but pursue
> Inferior objects, weake and partiall."
>
>   (Ode **xxiv.**)

A second tenet of Platonism which was reworked into English love poetry was its con-

ception of love. As Spenser had explained in his " Hymne in Honour of Beautie," true love has its source in the life of two souls in heaven. (ll. 200–213.) Drummond uses the idea to explain the purity of his love.

> " That learned Grecian, who did so excel
>   In knowledge passing sense, that he is nam'd
> Of all the after-worlds divine, doth tell,
>   That at the time when first our souls are fram'd,
>   Ere in these mansions blind they come to dwell,
> They live bright rays of that eternal light,
> And others see, know, love, in heaven's great height,
>   Not toil'd with aught to reason doth rebel.
> Most true it is, for straight at the first sight
> My mind me told, that in some other place
> It elsewhere saw the idea of that face,
>   And lov'd a love of heavenly pure delight;
> No wonder now I feel so fair a flame,
> Sith I her lov'd ere on this earth she came."
>
> ("Poems." First Pt., S. vii.)

In Vaughan the same theory of love is again referred to as a proof of the poet's lofty passion. In "To Amoret. Walking in a Starry Evening," he says that even were her face a distant star shining upon him, he would be sure of a sympathy between it and himself, because their minds were united in love by no accident or chance of sight, but were designed for one another.

" But, Amoret, such is my fate,
  That if thy face a star
  Had shin'd from far,
I am persuaded in that state,
  'Twixt thee and me,
  Of some predestin'd sympathy.

" For sure such two conspiring minds,
  Which no accident, or sight,
  Did thus unite;
Whom no distance can confine
  Start, or decline,
  One for another were design'd."

          (Stzs. 3, 4.)

In a second lyric, " A Song to Amoret," he describes his love as superior to that which a " mighty amorist " could give, because it is a love that was born with his soul in heaven.

" For all these arts I'd not believe,
  — No, though he should be thine —
The mighty amorist could give
  So rich a heart as mine.

" Fortune and beauty thou might find,
  And greater men than I :
By my true resolvèd mind
  They never shall come nigh.

" For I not for an hour did love,
  Or for a day desire,
But with my soul had from above
  This endless, holy fire."

         (Stzs. 4–6.)

Thus far the tenets of Platonic theory have been used in a more or less direct way; but in several instances the Platonic idea is present only in the writer's mind, and the reader is left to unravel it by his own ingenuity. Thus Shakespeare urges his friend to marry because in his death truth and beauty will both end — a possible inference being that his friend is ideal beauty.

> " Not from the stars do I my judgment pluck;
> And yet methinks I have Astronomy,
> But not to tell of good, or evil luck,
> Of plagues, of dearths, or seasons' quality;
> Nor can I fortune to brief minutes tell,
> Pointing to each his thunder, rain and wind,
> Or say with Princes if it shall go well,
> By oft predict that I in heaven find:
> But from thine eyes my knowledge I derive,
> And, constant stars, in them I read such art
> As truth and beauty shall together thrive,
> If from thyself to store thou wouldst convert;
> Or else of thee this I prognosticate:
> Thy end is Truth's and Beauty's doom and date."
>
> (xiv.)

In another sonnet Shakespeare plays with words in an attempt to excuse his truant muse for not praising his friend's beauty. His muse may say that since his friend is true beauty he needs no praise.

" O truant Muse, what shall be thy amends
    For thy neglect of truth in beauty dyed?
    Both truth and beauty on my love depends;
    So dost thou too, and therein dignified.
    Make answer, Muse; wilt thou not haply say
    ' Truth needs no colour with his colour fix'd;
    Beauty no pencil, beauty's truth to lay;
    But best is best, if never intermix'd?'"

But so closely identified is the praise of his
friend's beauty with the immortality conferred
by poetry that Shakespeare cannot justly excuse
the silence of his muse

" Because he needs no praise, wilt thou be dumb?
    Excuse not silence so; for't lies in thee
    To make him much outlive a gilded tomb,
    And to be praised of ages yet to be."

(ci.)

Again, Shakespeare describes how, when absent
from his friend, he is able to play with the
flowers as shadows of his friend's beauty.

" They were but sweet, but figures of delight,
    Drawn after you, you pattern of all those.
    Yet seem'd it Winter still, and, you away,
    As with your shadow I with these did play."

(xcviii.)

In Spenser the lover is able to make an appeal for pity by reference to the Platonic conception of the idea of the beloved which the
lover is supposed to behold in his soul.

"Leave lady in your glasse of christall clene,
 your goodly selfe for evermore to vew;
 and in my selfe, my inward selfe, I meane,
 most lively lyke behold your semblant trew.
Within my hart, though hardly it can shew,
 thing so divine to vew of earthly eye:
 the fayre Idea of your celestiall hew,
 and every part remaines immortally:
And were it not that, through your cruelty,
 with sorrow dimmed and deformed it were:
 the goodly ymage of your visnomy,
 clearer than christall would therein appere.
But if your selfe in me ye playne will see,
 remove the cause by which your fayre beames dark-
  ened be."

            (xlv.)

The end which this conception of making
love after the manner of the Platonist served
was thought to be found in a purification of
love. By praising the beauty of the beloved in
such lofty terms the poet was able to set off
the purity of his love from any connection with
mere sensual desire. Thus Spenser testifies to
the ennobling power of the beauty of his beloved's eyes.

"More then most faire, full of the living fire
 Kindled above unto the maker neere:
 no eies but joyes, in which al powers conspire,
 that to the world naught else be counted deare.
Thrugh your bright beams doth not ye blinded guest,

shoot out his harts to base affections wound;
but Angels come to lead fraile mindes to rest
in chast desires on heavenly beauty bound.
You frame my thoughts and fashion me within,
you stop my toung, and teach my hart to speake,
you calme the storme that passion did begin,
strong thrugh your cause, but by your vertue weak.
Dark is the world, where your light shined never:
well is he borne that may behold you ever."

(viii.)

In Sidney there is a direct reference to the
power of Plato's thought to lead the mind
from the desire with which he is struggling.

"Your words, my freeuds me causelesly doe blame,
My young minde marde whom love doth menace so:
     *   *   *   *   *
That *Plato* I have reade for nought, but if he tame
Such coltish yeeres; that to my birth I owe
Nobler desires:"

(xxi.)

The application of the tenets of Platonic
theory to the writing of love lyrics in the Petrarchian manner, however, was never anything
more than a courtly way of making love through
exaggerated conceit and fine writing.   Fulke
Greville saw clearly the relation between the
love of woman and the love of the idea of her
beauty.   In the tenth sonnet of his " Cælica "

he asks what can love find in a mind where all
is passion; rather he says go back to

> "that heavenly quire
> Of Nature's riches, in her beauties placed,
> And there in contemplation feed desire,
> Which till it wonder, is not rightly graced;
> For those sweet glories, which you do aspire,
> Must, as idea's, only be embraced,
> Since excellence in other forme enjoyed,
> Is by descending to her saints destroyed."

The love of the idea of beauty, however, in its
absolute nature is nowhere present in the mass
of love lyrics written between 1590 and 1600.
The term is used to give title to Drayton's
"Idea," and to denominate the object of twelve
sonnets addressed by Craig to "Idea"; and ana-
grams on the French word for the term L'Idée,
Diella and Delia, are used to name two series
of poems by Linche and Samuel Daniel, respectively. Crashaw's "Wishes" is addressed to "his
(supposed) mistresse," as an idea. No better
commentary on the whole movement can be
made than these words of Spenser in which it is
easily seen how the method conduced only to
feeding the lower desires of the soul in love.
Writing in 1596, in the midst of the period

when sonnet writing was most popular in England, he says, speaking of his two "Hymnes":

"Having in the greener times of my youth,
composed these former two Hymnes in the
praise of Love and beautie, and finding that the
same too much pleased those of like age and
disposition, which being too vehemently caried
with that kind of affection, do rather sucke out
poyson to their strong passion, then hony to
their honest delight, I was moved . . . to call
in the same. But being unable so to doe, by
reason that many copies thereof were formerly
scattered abroad, I resolved at least to amend,
and by way of retraction to reforme them, making in stead of those two Hymnes of earthly or
naturall love and beautie, two others of heavenly
and celestiall."

The great representative of Platonism in
English poetry thus condemns the less vital
phase of Platonic thought. The great weak-
ness of the theory lay in the fact that it had no
moral significance ; and just here lay the
great strength of Plato's ethics. Although
preaching that beauty was a spiritual thing,
this phase of Platonic æsthetics never blended
with the conception of the beauty of moral

goodness. And it failed to do this because it is a theory not of Plato but of Plotinus, who throughout the period of the Renaissance was understood to expound the true meaning of Plato's thought. But Plato left no system of æsthetics; Plotinus, however, constructed a theory to account for beauty in its strictest sense. Now Ficino in his propaganda of Platonic theory throughout the Renaissance interpreted Plato's " Symposium " in the light of Plotinus and thus in his commentary, the source of all Renaissance theorizing on love, is found the theory reflected in the English poets. This fusion of Plato's ethics with the æsthetics of Plotinus was not perfect; and to the deep moral genius of Spenser's mind the disparity soon became evident.

The Platonic theory of love had enabled the English poets to write about their passion as a desire of enjoying the spiritual quality of beauty in their beloved. In those poets in whom the Petrarchistic manner is evident, it is the object of love on which the attention centres; only in a slight way did they treat of the nature of love as a passion. The result of the discussion of love, as opened by Platonism, ended, however, in an attempt to place love upon a purely spiritual basis and to write about it as if it were a psychological fact that was to be known by analysis. A consideration of beauty, as the object of love, is absent ; attention is directed to the quality of the passion as one felt in the soul rather than by the sense ; and when the attraction of woman is present in this love it is carefully differentiated from the attraction of sex. In the body of love lyrics written in the seventeenth century the distinctive traits of this passion are clearly explained.

The chief trait of this kind of love is that it concerns only the soul. The union of the lover and the beloved is simply a union of their souls which because of the high nature of the soul can triumph over time and space. The character of this union is described in Donne's " Ecstacy." The two lovers are described as sitting in silence, watching one another. While thus engaged their souls are so mysteriously mingled that they are mixed into one greater soul which is not subject to change. Even when the passion descends from this height to the plane of human affections there is no essential change in the purity of the love.

" Where, like a pillow on a bed,
     A pregnant bank swell'd up, to rest
The violet's reclining head,
     Sat we two, one another's best.

*   *   *   *   *

" As, 'twixt two equal armies, Fate
     Suspends uncertain victory,
Our souls — which to advance their state,
     Were gone out — hung 'twixt her and me.

*   *   *   *   *

" This ecstacy doth unperplex
     (We said), and tell us what we love ;
We see by this, it was not sex ;
     We see, we saw not, what did move :

" But as all several souls contain
     Mixture of things they know not what,
Love these mix'd souls doth mix again,
     And makes both one, each this, and that.

*   *   *   *   *

" When love with one another so
     Interanimates two souls,
That abler soul, which thence doth flow,
     Defects of loneliness controls.

" We then, who are this new soul, know,
     Of what we are composed, and made,
For th' atomies of which we grow
     Are souls, whom no change can invade.

*   *   *   *   *

" And if some lover, such as we
    Have heard this dialogue of one,
Let him still mark us, he shall see
    Small change when we're to bodies gone."

In a like strain Randolph in "A Platonic Elegy"
praises his love as that founded on reason, not
on sense. The true union in love, he says, is
the meeting of essence with essence.

" Thus they, whose reasons love, and not their sense,
    The spirits love; thus one intelligence
Reflects upon his like, and by chaste loves
In the same sphere this and that angel moves.

          *   *   *   *   *

" When essence meets with essence, and souls join
    In mutual knots, that's the true nuptial twine.
Such, lady, is my love, and such is true :
All other love is to your sex, not you."
                                   (ll. 31–34, 45–48.

The great value which this purely spiritual
love was supposed to possess was that it was
unaffected either by time or distance.   The
union, not being one known to sense, could
exist as well in the absence of the lovers as in
the presence of both.   This thought is a great
comfort and is emphasized as the peculiarity in
the lovers' passion that sets it apart from the

vulgar kind.   Thus Donne in the song, "Soul's
Joy," consoles his beloved with the assurance
that their souls may meet though their bodies
be absent.

> "Soul's joy, now I am gone,
>   And you alone,
>   — Which cannot be,
> Since I must leave myself with thee,
>   And carry thee with me —
> Yet when unto our eyes
>   Absence denies
>   Each other's sight,
> And makes to us a constant night,
>   When others change to light;
>   *O give no way to grief,*
>   *But let belief*
>   *Of mutual love*
> *This wonder to the vulgar prove,*
>   *Our bodies, not we move.*
>
>
> "Let not thy wit beweep
>   Words but sense deep;
>   For when we miss
> By distance our hope's joining bliss
>   Even then our souls shall kiss;
>   Fools have no means to meet,
>   But by their feet;
>   Why should our clay
> Over our spirits so much sway,
>   To tie us to that way?
>   *O give no way to grief, etc.*"

In his " Valediction Forbidding Mourning,"
Donne again recurs to the subject of separation
and explains by the figure of the compass how
their souls will be one.   The love in which the
mind is bent on the objects of sense cannot
admit of absence ; but the love shared by
Donne and his mistress is so refined that their
souls suffer only an expansion and not separation in absence.

" Dull sublunary lover's love
   — Whose soul is sense — cannot admit
Of absence, 'cause it doth remove
   The thing which elemented it.

" But we by a love so far refined,
   That ourselves know not what it is,
Inter-assurèd of the mind,
   Care less eyes, lips and hands to miss.

"Our two souls therefore, which are one,
   Though I must go, endure not yet
A breach, but an expansion,
   Like gold to airy thinness beat.

" If they be two, they are two so
   As stiff twin compasses are two ;
Thy soul, the fix'd foot, makes no show
   To move, but doth, if th' other do.

" And though it in the centre sit,
    Yet, when the other far doth roam,
It leans, and hearkens after it,
    And grows erect, as that comes home."

                                    (Stzs. 4–8.)

Even in death this love will still live. Thus
Lord Herbert explains that his love has passed
over into that of the soul, and it will be as immortal as the soul.

" But since I must depart, and that our love
Springing at first but in an earthly mould
Transplanted to our souls, now doth remove
Earthly affects, which time and distance would,
        Nothing now can our loves allay,
            Though as the better Spirits will,
            That both love us and know our ill,
        We do not either all the good we may.
Thus when our Souls that must immortal be,
    For our loves cannot die, nor we (unless
We die not both together) shall be free
Unto their open and eternal peace.
        Sleep, Death's Embassador, and best
            Image, doth yours often so show,
            That I thereby must plainly know,
        Death unto us must be freedom and rest." [1]

The second characteristic of this love is that
it is purely contemplative, informing the mind
with knowledge rather than satisfying the

[1] " Poems of Lord Herbert of Cherbury," ed. John Churton Collins, p. 24.

senses with pleasure. Habington has left a
poem entitled " To the World. The Perfection of Love," in which he contrasts this love in
which the soul is engaged with thoughts with
the love of sense.

> " You who are earth, and cannot rise
>   Above your sence,
>   Boasting the envyed wealth which lyes
>   Bright in your mistris' lips or eyes,
>   Betray a pittyed eloquence.

> " That, which doth joyne our soules, so light
>   And quicke doth move,
>   That, like the eagle in his flight,
>   It doth transcend all humane sight,
>   Lost in the element of love.

> " You poets reach not this, who sing
>   The praise of dust
>   But kneaded, when by theft you bring
>   The rose and lilly from the spring,
>   T' adorne the wrinckled face of lust.

> " When we speake love, nor art, nor wit
>   We glosse upon :
>   Our soules engender, and beget
>   Ideas which you counterfeit
>   In your dull propagation.

> " While time seven ages shall disperse,
>   Wee'le talke of love,
>   And when our tongues hold no commerse,

> Our thoughts shall mutually converse ;
> And yet the blood no rebell provo.

> " And though we be of severall kind,
>   Fit for offence :
> Yet are we so by love refin'd,
> From impure drosse we are all mind,
>   Death could not more have conquer'd sence."

By virtue of this contemplation in love the
passion was freed from any disturbing element
due to absence, just as the restriction of love
to the soul had been thought to do. Vaughan
boasts to Amoret that he can dispense with a
sight of her face or with a kiss because when
absent from her he can court the mind.

> " Just so base, sublunary lovers' hearts
>   Fed on loose profane desires,
>   May for an eye
>   Or face comply :
> But those remov'd, they will as soon depart,
>   And show their art,
>   And painted fires.

> " Whilst I by pow'rful love, so much refin'd,
>   That my absent soul the same is,
>   Careless to miss
>   A glance or kiss,
> Can with these elements of lust and sense
>   Freely dispense,
>   And court the mind."

In the examples thus far given, the character of the passion as shared by lover and beloved has been merely described.   There was an attempt made in some of this poetry to define love as if it were a something to be analyzed — a product, as it were, of psychological elaboration. Vaughan has indicated the two traits in the love lyrist of the seventeenth century, when he gives the following title to a lyric, — " To Amoret, of the Difference 'Twixt Him and Other Lovers, and What True Love Is." In defining " What True Love Is," the poets show that it cannot be desire, but is rather an essence pure in itself, and in one instance it is described as something unknowable either to sense or to mind.

Donne has left a letter in verse " To the Countess of Huntingdon," in which he carefully explains how love cannot be desire.   Sighing and moaning may be love, but it is love made in a weak way ; love should never cast one down, but should elevate.

> " I cannot feel the tempest of a frown;
> I may be raised by love, but not thrown **down**;
> Though I can pity those sigh twice a **day**,
> I hate that thing whispers itself away.

> Yet since all love is fever, who to trees
> Doth talk, doth yet in love's cold ague freeze.
> 'Tis love, but with such fatal weakness made,
> That it destroys itself with its own shade."
>
> (ll. 27-34.)

At first love was mere desire, ignorant of its object; but now love is a matter of the soul, and it is profane to call rages of passion love.

> " As all things were one nothing, dull and weak,
> Until this raw disorder'd heap did break,
> And several desires led parts away,
> Water declined with earth, the air did stay,
> Fire rose, and each from other but untied,
> Themselves unprison'd were and purified;
> So was love, first in vast confusion hid,
> An unripe willingness which nothing did,
> A thirst, an appetite which had no ease,
> That found a want, but knew not what would please.
> What pretty innocence in those days moved!
> Man ignorantly walk'd by her he loved;
> Both sigh'd and interchanged a speaking eye;
> Both trembled and were sick : both knew not why."
>
> (ll. 37-51.)

This state may well become this early age, but now

> " passion is to woman's love, about,
> Nay, farther off, than when we first set out.
> It is not love that sueth, or doth contend;
> Love either conquers, or but meets a friend;
> Man's better part consists of purer fire,
> And finds itself allow'd, ere it desire."
>
> (ll. 55-60.)

The reason for this lies in the fact that love begins in the soul, and not in the sight.

> " He much profanes whom valiant heats do move
> To style his wandering rage of passion, Love.
> Love that imparts in everything delight,
> Is fancied in the soul, not in the sight."
>   (ll. 125–128.)

In Jonson's "Epode" in "The Forest," the same differentiation of love from passion is present, and an attempt is made to define love as an essence. The love of the present is nothing but raging passion.

> " The thing they here call Love, is blind desire,
> Arm'd with bow, shafts, and fire;
> Inconstant, like the sea, of whence 'tis born,
> Rough, swelling, like a storm."

True love, however, is an essence, a calmness, a peace.

> " Now, true love
> No such effects doth prove;
> That is an essence far more gentle, fine,
> Pure, perfect, nay divine;
> * * * * *
> this bears no brands, nor darts,
> To murder different hearts,
> But in a calm, and godlike unity,
> Preserves community."

In Donne in his "Love's Growth," there is an expression of doubt whether his love can be as

pure as he thought it was, because it seems to
suffer an increase in the spring, and is not a
thing without component elements. But if love
is no quintessence, he says, it must be mixed
with alien passions and thus not be pure. He
silences his doubts, however, by explaining
after the analogy of concentric rings of waves
of water about the centre of disturbance how
his love is one and unelemented.

> " I scarce believe my love to be so pure
>   As I had thought it was,
>   Because it doth endure
>   Vicissitude, and season, as the grass;
>   Methinks I lied all winter, when I swore
>   My love was infinite, if spring make it more.
>
> " But if this medicine, love, which cures all sorrow
>   With more, not only be no quintessence,
>   But mix'd of all stuffs, vexing soul, or sense,
>   And of the sun his active vigour borrow,
>
> " Love's not so pure, and abstract as they use
>   To say, which have no mistress but their Muse;
>   But as all else, being elemented too,
>   Love sometimes would contemplate, sometimes do.
>
> *   *   *   *   *
>
> " If, as in water stirr'd more circles be
>   Produced by one, love such additions take,
>   Those like so many spheres but one heaven make,
>   For they are all concentric unto thee."

(I. 34, 35.)

Again, in "The Dream," he fears the strength
of his beloved's affection if it is mingled with
a sense of fear, or shame, or honor.

> "That love is weak where fear's as strong as he;
> T'is not all spirit, pure and brave,
> If mixture it of fear, shame, honour have;"
>
> (I. 39.)

This refinement of the subject of love is
carried to an even greater excess. Love is such
a passion that it can be defined only by nega-
tives. It is above apprehension, because sense
and soul both can know the object of their love.
In the poem of Donne's "Negative Love," in
which this idea is expressed, it is probable that
the poet has in mind the description of The
One which Plotinus outlines in the "Enneads."
Summing up his discussion of The One, or The
Good, in which he has pointed out how it is
above intellect, Plotinus says: "If, however,
anything is present with *the good*, it is present
with it in a way transcending knowledge and
intelligence and a cosensation of itself, since it
has not anything different from itself. . . .
On this account says Plato [in the "Parmeni-
des," speaking of *the one*] that neither language
can describe, nor sense nor science apprehend

it, because nothing can be predicated of it as
present with it." (" Enneads," VI. vii. 41.)
Transferring this idea of the transcendency of
The One to his love, Donne had the form of
thought for his lyric.

> " I never stoop'd so low, as they
>   Which on an eye, cheek, lip, can prey;
>   Seldom to them which soar no higher
>   Than virtue, or the mind to admire.
>   For sense and understanding may
>   Know what gives fuel to their fire;
>   My love, though silly, is more brave;
>   For may I miss whene'er I crave,
>   If I know yet what I would have.
>
> " If that be simply perfectest,
>   Which can by no way be express'd
>   But negatives, my love is so.
>   To all, which all love, I say no.
>   If any who deciphers best,
>   What we know not — ourselves — can know,
>   Let him teach me that nothing.   This
>   As yet my ease and comfort is,
>   Though I speed not, I cannot miss."

This reference to the knowledge of self also
occurs in Plotinus in the preceding sentence
to the passage already extracted. " For the
mandate," he says, " ' know thyself,' was de-
livered to those, *who, on account of the multitude*

which they possess, find it requisite to enumer-
ate themselves, and in order that by knowing
the number and quality of the things contained
in their essence, they may perceive that they
have not a knowledge of all things, or, indeed,
of anything [which they ought to know], and
who are ignorant over what they ought to rule,
and what is the characteristic of their nature."
(VI. vii. 41.)

This highly metaphysical conception of love,
the character of which has been shown in a few
selected examples, became in the course of
time known as "Platonic Love." Scattered
throughout the lyric poetry of the seventeenth
century may be found certain poems labelled
"Platonic Love." Their presence among the
author's work is no testimony whatsoever that
it is colored by any strain of Platonism, but
merely signifies that at one time in his career
the poet wrote love lyrics according to the
prevailing manner of the time. For about
1634 Platonic love was a court fad. Howell,
writing under date of June 3, 1634, says: "The
Court affords little News at present, but that
there is a Love call'd Platonick Love which
much sways there of late: it is a Love ab-

stracted from all corporeal gross Impressions
and sensual Appetite, but consists in Contem-
plations and Ideas of the Mind, not in any
carnal Fruition.   This Love sets the Wits of
the Town on work ; and they say there will be
a Mask shortly of it, whereof Her Majesty and
her Maids of Honour will be part." [1]

The masque referred to is D'Avenant's " The
Temple of Love " (1634).   In Thomas Heywood's
"Love's Mistress or the Queen's Masque" (1640)
the myth of Cupid and Psyche is interpreted in
accordance with the notion of Platonic love ;
and in D'Avenant's " Platonick Lovers " (1636)
the subject of Platonic love is ridiculed.   It is
probable that the rise of this custom at the court
was due to the presence of Henrietta Maria, the
queen of Charles I.   Margaret of Valois had
made Platonic love known in France ; and had
shown how licentiousness of conduct was com-
patible with its practice.   " She had a high
harmonious soul," writes Howell,[2] " much ad-
dicted to music and the sweets of love, and
oftentimes in a Platonic way ; She would have
this Motto often in her mouth ; *Voulez vous*

---

[1] Howell's " Letters," Bk. I, sect. 6, let. XV.
[2] " Lustra Ludovicii," p. 26.   London, 1646.

cesser d'aymer? possedez la chose aymée. . . .
She had strains of humors and transcendencies
beyond the vulgar, and delighted to be call'd
Venus Urania." It is probable that the young
queen wished to follow such an example and
made known to the English court this new
way of love gallantry. The practice of making love in the Platonic way grew so popular
at any rate as to become a question of serious
discussion. John Norris says, "*Platonic Love* is
a thing in every Bodies Mouth," and after com-
paring it with the love described by Plato in
the "Symposium," he concludes, "But why
this should be call'd by the name of *Platonic*
Love, the best reason that I know of, is because
People will have it so." [1] Algernon Sidney has
left an account of love as a desire of enjoying
beauty. He concludes that since man is mid-
way between angels and beasts, his love will
share in the peculiarities of both the celestial
and the sensual passion.[2] Walter Charleton
ridicules the subject and unmasks its immorality, although his purpose is not in any way to

[1] " An Account of Plato's Ideas, and of Platonic Love."
"Miscellanies," pp. 355–364.
[2] " An Essay on Love," p. 275.

purify the morals of his readers.[1] Robert Boyle
wrote, but did not publish, a series of letters,
"wherein [among other subjects] Platonic love
was explicated, celebrated, and wherein the cure
of love was proposed and prosecuted."[2]

The ideas expressed in these poems on Platonic love are not essentially different from
those in the lyrics which have been already
discussed. At times, as in Stanley's "Love's
Innocence," the Platonic manner is understood
as one devoid of all danger. It was in this
way that Vaughan looked upon his love for
Amoret. "You have here," he says, "a
flame, bright only in its own innocence, that
kindles nothing but a generous thought, which
though it may warm the blood, the fire at
highest is but Platonic; and the commotion,
within these limits, excludes danger."[3] On the
other hand, Carew's "Song to a Lady, not yet
Enjoyed by her Husband," shows how the stock
ideas was used to cloak the immorality of the
poet's thought. George Daniel has left a series

[1] "The Ephesian and Cimmerian Matrons," 1668.

[2] "A Treatise of Seraphic Love." Advertisements to the
Reader, p. 12.

[3] "Poems, with the Tenth Satire of Juvenal Englished,
1646." Preface.

of poems revealing the several phases of this love ranging between the two extremes. He writes one " To Cinthia, coying it," in which its innocence is preached. " To Cinthia Converted " describes the union of the two souls. " To the Platonicke Pretender " warns the ladies from listening to this love when taught by a libertine. " Pure Platonicke " explains the spiritual nature of the passion by contrast with sensual love. " Court-Platonicke " shows how at court it was used merely as a means to an improper end. " Anti-Platonicke " recites the feelings of the sensual lover.[1] In Lord Herbert are found two other phases of this love. The first and second of his poems named " Platonick Love " are complimentary poems addressed to a lady ; the first, telling her how the love inspired by her refines his soul, and the second celebrating Platonic love in general application.

> " For as you can unto that height refine
> All Loves delights, as while they do incline
> Unto no vice, they so become divine,
> We may as well attain your excellence,
> As, without help of any outward sense
> Would make us grow a pure Intelligence."
>
> (Stz. 2.)

[1] Works, ed. Grosart, I. 112-123.

In the third "Platonicke Love" the lover is
represented as wavering between despair and
hope with a slight balance in favor of the latter.
He is disconsolate because he finds no hope

> "when my matchless Mistress were inclin'd
> To pity me, 'twould scarcely make me glad,
> The discomposing of so fair a mind
> Being that which would to my Affections add."
>
> (Stz. 1.)

He finds hope, however, in the thought that

> "though due merit I cannot express,
> Yet she shall know none ever lov'd for less
> Or easier reward. Let her remain
> Still great and good, and from her Happiness
> My chief contentment I will entertain."
>
> (Stz. 7.)

He ends with hope still living:

> "Then, hope, sustain thy self: though thou art hid
> Thou livest still, and must till she forbid;
> For when she would my vows and love reject,
> They would a Being in themselves project,
> Since infinites as they yet never did,
> Nor could conclude without some good effect."
>
> (Stz. 16.)

Platonic love, as such an example proves, was
but synonymous with hopeless love.

Platonic love, then, meant either a love devoid of all sensual desire, an innocent or hope-

less passion, or it was a form of gallantry used
to cloak immorality.   Its one characteristic
notion was that true love consisted in a union
of soul with soul, mind with mind, or essence
with essence.   This idea of restricting love to
the experience of soul as opposed to the enjoyment of sense is the one notion which runs beneath many of the love lyrics written in the
seventeenth century; and it is the point at-
tacked by opponents.   In John Cleveland, " To
Cloris, a Rapture," and in Campion's " Song " [1]
the poets exhort their beloved to enjoy this
high union of soul.   In Carew's " To My Mistress in Absence," in Lovelace's " To Lucasta.
Going beyond the Seas," and in Cowley's
" Friendship in Absence," the triumph of love
over time and space is explained by the mingling of souls in true love.   In Sedley's " The
Platonick " and in Ayres's " Platonic Love "
are found examples of the hopelessness of the
passion.   In Aytoun's " Platonic Love " which
was taken by Suckling to form a poem — the
" Song," beginning, " If you refuse me once " —
the lover modestly confesses that he cannot
rise to the heights of such a pure passion, and

[1] Works, ed. A. H. Bullen, p. 124.

requests a more easy way. In Cleveland's
"The Anti-Platonick" and "Platonick Love,"
in Brome's "Epithalamy," in Cowley's "Platonick Love" and "Answer to the Platonicks,"
and in Cartwright's "No Platonique Love," the
claims of the opponents are expressed in all the
grossness of Restoration immorality.

The atmosphere in which the metaphysical
treatment of love flourished was intensely intellectual. The poets in whom the strain is
clearest were trying to accomplish two things :
they wished to oppose the idea of passion in
love, and they endeavored to account for the
attraction of sex in the love which they themselves experienced. However much these poets
wished to exclude the notion of sex, their minds
were constantly busied in trying to solve the
source of its power. In Donne, the greatest
representative of the metaphysical manner, this
purpose is very evident. He wrote his long-
est poem, "An Anatomy of the World," to
show how, by reason of the death of a certain
young woman, "the frailty and the decay of
this whole world is represented." In reply to
Jonson's criticism, that this poem was "full of
blasphemies," Donne remarked that "he de-

scribed the Idea of a Woman, and not as she was." [1] Here lies the secret of Donne's treatment of woman ; he was interested in her, not as a personality, but as an idea. In solving the nature of this idea he recurred to certain Platonic conceptions by which he thought to explain the source of her power.

These Platonic conceptions are two. Woman is identified with virtue ; she is the source of all virtue in the world, others being virtuous only by participating in her virtue. Thus in a letter "To the Countess of Huntingdon" he shows how virtue has been raised from her fallen state on earth by appearing in woman. She was once scattered among men, but now summed up in one woman.

" If the world's age and death be argued well
    By the sun's fall, which now towards earth doth bend,
Then we might fear that virtue, since she fell
    So low as woman, should be near her end.

" But she's not stoop'd, but raised ; exiled by men
    She fled to heaven, that's heavenly things, that's
      you ;
She was in all men thinly scatter'd then,
    But now a mass contracted in a few.

[1] " Ben Jonson's Conversations with William Drummond," p. 3. Shakespeare's Soc. Pub. v. 8.

" She gilded us, but you are gold; and she
    Informed us, but transubstantiates you.
Soft dispositions, which ductile be,
    Elixirlike, she makes not clean, but new.

" Though you a wife's and mother's name retain,
    'Tis not as woman, for all are not so;
But virtue, having made you virtue, is fain
    To adhere in these names, her and you to show.

" Else, being alike pure, we should neither see;
    As, water being into air rarefied,
Neither appear, till in one cloud they be,
    So, for our sakes, you do low names abide."

Beneath this torture of conceits may be seen
the idea that woman is that very virtue of
which Plato has spoken in his " Phædrus."
Sidney has used the idea to compliment Stella;
but Donne's purpose is to show how woman, as
woman, is to be identified with it, and that the
differentiation in the concept resulting from
the fact that she may be a wife or a mother is
due to the necessity that this virtue become
visible on earth.

The second Platonic conception through
which Donne conveys his idea of woman's
nature is the universal soul. In his lyric, " A
Fever," he says, speaking of the object of his
love :

" But yet thou canst not die, I know;
    To leave this world behind, is death;
    But when thou from this world wilt go,
    The whole world vapours with thy breath.

" Or if, when thou, the world's soul, go'st
    It stay, 'tis but thy carcase then."

And in " An Anatomy of the World " this idea
of the death of the world in the death of a
woman is explained at length.

Holding thus to this idea of woman, and striving to differentiate love from passion, Donne
was able to confine his notion of love to the
soul; and through the metaphysical manner of
his poetic art he was able to express this notion
in the most perplexing intricacies of thought.
As Dryden has said, " he affects the metaphysics, not only in his satires, but in his amorous
verses, where nature only should reign : and
perplexes the minds of the fair sex with the
speculations of philosophy, where he should
engage their hearts, and entertain them with
the softness of love." [1] By imitating his style
the other lyric poets of the seventeenth century
produced the species of love poems which have

---

[1] Works, ed. Saintsbury, xi. 124, note.

already been analyzed. His skill and his sincerity of aim are lacking in their verse; and the result was either a weak dilution of his thought or a striving for his manner in praising a lower conception of love.

CHAPTER III

GOD AND THE SOUL

I. NATURE OF GOD

PLATONISM affected Christian theology as it
appears in English poetry in a twofold way.
It provided a body of intellectual principles
which were identified with the persons of the
Christian Trinity and it also trained the minds
of the poets in conceiving God rather as the
object of the mind's speculative quest than as
the dread judge of the sinful soul. Platonism
in this form is no longer the body of ethical
principles appearing in the Platonic dialogues;
but is that metaphysical after-growth of Platonism that has its source in the philosophy of
Plotinus. According to this form of speculative mysticism there were three ultimate principles, or hypostases, — The Good, Intellect ($\nu o\hat{v}s$),
and Soul. Owing to the affinity of Platonism
for Christian forms of thought, these three

167

hypostases were conceived as the philosophic
basis underlying the Christian teaching of the
three Persons of the Trinity. Such an interpretation is seen plainly in the work of Henry
More and William Drummond ; and the speculative attitude of conceiving God and Christ in
the light of the hypostases of Plotinus is also
discernible in Spenser and Milton.

The boldest attempt to identify the three
Plotinian principles with the Christian Trinity
is made in Henry More's " Psychozoia," the
first poem of his " Psychodia Platonica." This
poetical treatise reveals the aim of More's
spiritual life as it was formulated on the basis
of Platonic philosophy blended with the teaching of the " Theologia Germanica." The
strain of self-abnegation which More learned in
"that *Golden little Book*," [1] as he names the
German treatise, may be easily separated from
the Platonism, being confined to the last two
books of his poem ; it may thus be dismissed.
In the first book, however, the current of
thought is almost purely Platonic. There,
under the figure of the marriage rite, the first
principle of Plotinus, the Good, is represented

[1] " Life of Henry More," Richard Ward, p. 12.

as joining his two children — Intellect and
Soul — in holy union ; and under the poetic
device of a veil with several films or tissues,
More describes Soul in minute detail.

In keeping with the teachings of Platonism
More defines each person of the Trinity in the
terms used by Plotinus. According to this
philosopher the highest reality is The One or
The Good which is infinite and above all com-
prehension, not because it is impossible to
measure or count it (since it has no magnitude
and no multitude), but simply because it is impossible to conceive its power. (" Enneads," VI.
ix. 6.) In the beatific vision, in which The Good
is known in the Soul, it is invisible, hidden in its
own rays of light. (" Enneads," VI. vii. 35.)
More thus speaks of God, naming him Hattove :

> " Th' Ancient of dayes, sire of *Æternitie*,
>   Sprung of himself, or rather nowise sprong.
>   Father of lights, and everlasting glee
>   Who puts to silence every daring tongue
>   And flies mans sight, shrouding himself among
>   His glorious rayes, good *Hattove*, from whom came
>   All good that *Penia* [*i.e.* want] spies in thickest throng
>   Of most desired things, all's from that same."
>   (I. 5.)
>   " But first of all
>   Was mighty *Hattove*, deeply covered o're

With unseen light.   No might Imaginall
May reach that vast profunditie."

(I. 16.)

The Son is identified with the second hypostasis, — universal intellect.   In this all realities
are present not as created things in time or
space, but embraced as essential forms with no
spatial or temporal relation.   This character of
universal intellect is thus named *αἰών*, or eternity.   (" Enneads," III. vii. 4.)   More thus
writes of Christ —

" The youthfull *Æon*, whose fair face doth shine
  While he his Fathers glory doth espy,
  Which waters his fine flowring forms with light from
    high.

" Not that his forms increase, or that they die.
  For *Æon Land*, which men *Idea* call,
  Is nought but life in full serenitie,
  Vigour of life is root, stock, branch, and all ;
  Nought here increaseth, nought here hath its fall;
  For *Æons* kingdomes alwaies perfect stand,
  Birds, beasts, fields, springs, plants, men and minerall,
  To perfectnesse nought added be there can."

(I. 13. 14.)

Psyche, or Uranore, as she is named at times,
is the third person of the Trinity.   She is the
soul of the universe, present in every " atom
ball," in the creatures of earth, sea, air, the

divine stars in heaven.   (" Enneads," V. i. 2.)
In her true essence she is invisible ; but More
pictures her as enveloped in a fourfold garment.   The outer garment is called Physis,
in which all natural objects appear as spots
which grow each according to its idea.   This
robe is stirred with every impulse of life from
the central power of God.

> " The first of these fair films, we *Physis* name.
> Nothing in nature did you ever spy
> But there's pourtraid :
>
>   *   *   *   *   *
>
> " And all besprinkeled with centrall spots,
> Dark little spots, is this hid inward veil.
>
>   *   *   *   *   *
>
> " When they dispread themselves, then gins to swell
> Dame *Psyches* outward vest, as th' inward wind
> Softly gives forth, full softly doth it well
> Forth from the centrall spot ;
>
>   *   *   *   *   *
>
>   according to the imprest Art
> (That Arts impression's from *Idea Land*)
> So drives it forth before it every part
> According to true symmetry. "   (I. 41–44.)

The second and third folds of Psyche's vest
are very closely identified.   They are called
Arachnea and Haphe, by which the life of

sensation is meant. Haphe, or touch, sits in the finely spun web of Arachnea, and is aware of every manifestation of life resulting from the soul's contact with the outward world. In this life of sensation Psyche sees as in a mirror all the stirring life within the universe. (I. 48, 49, 50.)

The fourth fold of Psyche's garment is called Semele, by which imagination is meant. This is the loosest of the four veils, having the fullest play in its movements. It is universal imagination, and from it arises the inspiration of the poet and the prophet. (I. 57.) The individual powers of imagination are conceived as daughters of the one great Semele.

> " She is the mother of each *Semele:*
>   The daughters be divided one from one;
>   But she grasps all. How can she then but see
>   Each *Semels* shadows by this union?
>   She sees and swayes imagination
>   As she thinks good: and it that she think good
>   She lets it play by 't self, yet looketh on,
>   While she keeps in that large strong-beating flood
>   That gars the Poet write, and rave as he were wood."
>   (I. 59.)

These three persons — Ahad, another name given by More to God (I. 34), Æon, and Psyche

— form, says More, "the famous Platonicall Triad ; which though they that slight the Christian Trinity do take for a figment; yet I think it is no contemptible argument, that the Platonists, the best and divinest of Philosophers, and the Christians, the best of all that do professe religion, do both concur that there is a Trinity. In what they differ, I leave to be found out, according to the safe direction of that infallible Rule of Faith, the holy Word." [1] To signify the union of these persons More represents Ahad joining Æon, his son, in marriage to Psyche, and by holding their hands in his, maintaining a perpetual unity.

"My first born Sonne, and thou my daughter dear,
Look on your aged Sire, the deep abysse,
In which and out of which you first appear ;
I *Ahad* hight, and *Ahad* onenesse is :
Therefore be one ; (his words do never misse)
They one became.

"They straight accord : then he put on the ring,
The ring of lasting gold on *Uranure ;*
Then gan the youthful Lads aloud to sing,
Hymen! O Hymen! O the Virgin pure!
O holy Bride! long may this joy indure.
(I. 34, 35.)

*　　*　　*　　*　　*

[1] "Psychozoia." To the Reader.

And all this time he held their hands in one;
Then they with chearfull look one thing desired,
That he nould break this happy union.
I happy union break? quoth he anon:
I *Ahad?* Father of Community?
Then they: That you nould let your hand be gone
Off from our hands. He grants with smiling glee."

(I. 38.)

In this way More has expressed his conception of the Christian Trinity. Inasmuch as his
purpose in the "Psychozoia" is to relate the
experiences of the human soul from the time
of its departure from God to its return thither,
he has laid especial emphasis upon the third
hypostasis of Plotinus, — Soul.

In William Drummond's "An Hymn of the
Fairest Fair" attention is centred upon the
first person of the Trinity. Drummond is
more of a poet and less of a philosopher than
More; but the philosophic conceptions which
are woven into his poetical description of the
nature, attributes, and works of God are drawn
from the same system of metaphysics. In
Drummond's "Hymn" there is a mingling of
two conceptions of God. He is described, according to the Hebraic idea, as a mighty king,
the creator of the universe, dwelling in heaven,

and possessing such attributes of personality
as justice, mercy, might. Running in and out
of this description is a strain of Platonic speculation, in which the conception of God as an
essence is very prominent. Thus by means
of a poetic device picturing youth standing before God and pouring immortal nectar into His
cup, Drummond expresses the Platonic idea of
absolute oneness. And this idea is the attribute of God first set forth.

> "If so we may well say (and what we say,
> Here wrapt in flesh, led by dim reason's ray,
> To show by earthly beauties which we see,
> That spiritual excellence that shines in thee,
> Good Lord, forgive), not far from thy right side,
> With curled locks Youth ever doth abide ;
> Rose-cheeked Youth, who, garlanded with flowers
> Still blooming, ceaselessly unto thee pours
> Immortal nectar in a cup of gold,
> That by no darts of ages thou grow old,
> And, as ends and beginnings thee not claim,
> Successionless that thou be still the same."
>   (ll. 31–42.)

After a description of God's might, Drummond passes on to consider His truth, conceived as the Platonists conceived intellect,
embracing all reality as essential form. This

attribute is pictured as a mirror in which God
beholds all things.

> "With locks in waves of gold that ebb and flow
>   On ivory neck, in robes more white than snow,
>   Truth steadfastly before thee holds a glass,
>   Indent with gems, where shineth all that was,
>   That is, or shall be. Here, ere aught was wrought,
>   Thou knew all that thy pow'r with time forth brought,
>   And more, things numberless which thou couldst make,
>   That actually shall never being take:
> Here, thou behold'st thyself, and, strange, dost prove
> At once the beauty, lover, and the love."

(ll. 56–66.)

Platonic metaphysics are also present in
Drummond's account of the essential unity
persisting throughout the triplicity of Persons. Plotinus had held that The One caused
the mind or intellect, and that in turn caused
universal soul. The order, however, is not
one of time sequence, but merely a logical order
of causation. In this series of causation there
is no idea of a production as an act going out
of itself and forming another ; each producing
cause remains in its own centre; throughout the
series runs one cause or manifestation of life.
His favorite figures by which he explains this
idea are, first, that of an overflowing spring
which gives rise to a second and this to a third;

and, second, that of a sun with a central source
of light with its spreading rays. (" Enneads,"
V. ii. 1, 2.) Thus intellect is an irradiation of
The One and soul is an irradiation of intellect.
(" Enneads," V. i. 6.) Drummond, holding to
the idea of the self-sufficiency of God as expressed in Plotinus, a state in which God is
alone by Himself and not in want of the things
that proceed from Him (" Enneads," VI. vii.
40), is thus able to unfold the mystery of the
One in Three :

" Ineffable, all-powrfull God, all free,
    Thou only liv'st, and each thing lives by thee ;
    No joy, no, nor perfection to thee came
    By the contriving of this world's great frame ;
            *   *   *   *   *
                    world nought to thee supplied,
    All in thyself thyself thou satisfied.
    Of good no slender shadow doth appear,
    No age-worn track, in thee which shin'd not clear ;
    Perfections sum, prime cause of every cause,
    Midst, end, beginning, where all good doth pause.
    Hence of thy substance, differing in nought,
    Thou in eternity, thy Son forth brought,
    The only birth of thy unchanging mind,
    Thine image, pattern-like that ever shin'd,
    Light out of light, begotton not by will,
    But nature, all and that same essence still
    Which thou thyself. . . .
            *   *   *   *   *

Of this light,
Eternal, double, kindled was thy spright
Eternally, who is with thee the same,
All-holy gift, ambassador, knot, flame.
Most sacred Triad! O most holy One!
Unprocreate Father, ever procreate Son,
Ghost breath'd from both, you were, are, aye shall be,
Most blessed, three in one, and one in three,
Incomprehensible by reachless height,
And unperceived by excessive light.

*   *   *   *   *

So, though unlike, the planet of the days,
So soon as he was made, begat his rays,
Which are his offspring, and from both was hurl'd
The rosy light which comfort doth the world,
And none forewent another ; so the spring
The well-head, and the stream which they forth bring,
Are but one selfsame essence, nor in aught
Do differ, save in order, and our thought
No chime of time discerns in them to fall,
But three distinctly bide one essence all."

(ll. 99–142.)

From this point on to the close, the " Hymn "
celebrates the glory of God in his works.
Drummond possessed an imagination that delighted as Milton's did in the contemplation of
the universe as a vast mechanical scheme of sun
and planets. (ll. 180–232.) His philosophic
mind, however, led him to conceive of nature
in the manner of the Platonists. God, or true

being, according to Plotinus is a unity, everywhere present ("Enneads," VI. v. 4); and
matter, the other extreme of his philosophy, is
an empty show, a shadow in a mirror. ("Enneads," III. vi. 7.) In closing the account of
the works of God, Drummond thus writes :

> "Whole and entire, all in thyself thou art,
> All-where diffus'd, yet of this All no part;
> For infinite, in making this fair frame,
> Great without quantity, in all thou came,
> And filling all, how can thy state admit
> Or place or substance to be.said of it?
>
> *   *   *   *   *
>
> Were but one hour this world disjoin'd from thee,
> It in one hour to nought reduc'd should be,
> For it thy shadow is; and can they last,
> If sever'd from the substances them cast?"

(ll. 285–298.)

Drummond's "Hymn" is the work of a mind
in which poetical sensuousness and philosophic
abstraction are well-nigh equally balanced. In
More the philosopher had outweighed the poet.
In Milton the poet asserts his full power. To
him the Plotinian scheme of the hypostases is
valuable only as they enable his love of beauty
to be satisfied in conformity with his intellectual apprehension of the relation between God
and the Son in the Trinal Godhead. Plotinus

had outlined the relation between The Good and Intellect as that of a principle of beauty by which the intellect is invested and possesses beauty and light. (" Enneads," VI. vii. 31.) The Good itself is the principle of beauty, hidden in its own rays of light. In Milton the conception of God as hidden in inaccessible light, and of the Son as the express image of the invisible beauty of God, is explained in conformity with the Platonic scheme, and also with those Scriptural texts, one of which mentions God as a King of kings, who only hath immortality, dwelling in the light which no man can approach unto (1 Tim. vi. 16) ; and the other proclaims that in Christ " dwelleth all the fulness of the Godhead bodily " (Col. ii. 9). Thus in heaven the angels hymn their praises :

" Thee, Father, first they sung, Omnipotent,
   Immutable, Immortal, Infinite,
   Eternal King ; thee, Author of all being,
   Fountain of light, thyself invisible
   Amidst the glorious brightness where thou sitt'st
   Throned inaccessible, but when thou shad'st
   The full blaze of thy beams, and through a cloud
   Drawn round about thee like a radiant shrine
   Dark with excessive bright thy skirts appear,
   Yet dazzle Heaven, that brightest Seraphim
   Approach not, but with both wings veil their eyes.

Thee next they sang, of all creation first,
Begotten Son, Divine Similitude,
In whose conspicuous countenance, without cloud
Made visible, the Almighty Father shines,
Whom else no creature can behold : on thee
Impressed the effulgence of his glory abides.
Transfused on thee his ample Spirit rests."

(P. L., III. 372–389.)

And the Almighty addresses the Son :

"'Effulgence of my glory, Son beloved,
Son in whose face invisible is beheld
Visibly, what by Deity I am.'"

(VI. 680–682.)

This relation of Christ to God which in the
Scripture was indicated only as in an outline
sketch has been filled in with the substance of
the Plotinian æsthetics, in which The One and
The Good is beauty itself (καλλονή) and intellect is the beautiful (τὸ καλόν). ("Enneads,"
I. vi. 6.)

The attraction which this philosophical explanation had for those whose work reveals its
presence is twofold. To the religious mind in
which the metaphysical cast of thought was
prominent, the idea of the transcendent immanence of God in all things as their life, yet apart
from all things as objects in time and space

came home with its wealth of suggestion of the
nearness of God to man.   In Henry More this
feeling is uppermost in his " Psychozoia."   In
the midst of his description of Psyche's robe
he breaks out into a passage on the constant
care which God shows toward the world.   In
Psyche's mirror of Arachnea and Haphe God
is aware of all on earth that falls under sense.
The roaring of the hungry lion, the burning
thirst of the weary traveller and every movement of the little sparrow are all known to him.

" Do not I see?   I slumber not nor sleep,
    Do not I heare? each noise by shady night
    My miroir represents : when mortals steep
    Their languid limbs in Morpheus dull delight,
    I hear such sounds as Adams brood would fright.
    The dolefull echoes from the hollow hill
    Mock houling wolves : the woods with black bedight.
    Answer rough Pan, his pipe and eke his skill,
    And all the Satyr-routs rude whoops and shoutings
        shrill."   (I. 54.)

In his second canto, where he repeats the idea
of the universal life of Psyche, he dwells on the
fact of God's immanence in the world.   He is
the inmost centre of creation, from whom as
rays from the sun the individual souls are
born.

" Dependence of this All hence doth appear
And severall degrees subordinate.
But phansie's so unfit such things to clear,
That oft it makes them seem more intricate ;
And now Gods work it doth disterminate
Too far from his own reach : But he withall
More inward is, and far more intimate
Then things are with themselves. His ideall
And centrall presence is in every atom-ball."
(II. 10.)

In those minds less metaphysical in nature,
the high speculations of Platonic philosophy
opened a way by which they could conceive
God as a principle grasped by the mind rather
than as a personal judge and punisher of sin.
In Drummond this contrast in the two conceptions of God — one feeding itself on philosophy, and the other on the imagery of the
Scripture — is strikingly brought out by a comparison of the opening and the ending of " An
Hymn of the Fairest Fair " with those of " A
Prayer for Mankind." The " Hymn " begins
with a confession of the elevating power of his
subject :

" I feel my bosom glow with wontless fires
  Rais'd from the vulgar press my mind aspires,
  Wing'd with high thoughts, unto his praise to climb,
  From deep eternity who called forth time;

That essence which not mov'd makes each thing move,
Uncreate beauty, all creating love:
But by so great an object, radiant light,
My heart appall'd, enfeebled rests my sight,
Thick clouds benight my labouring engine,
And at my high attempts my wits repine.
If thou in me this sacred rapture wrought,
My knowledge sharpen, sarcels [*i.e.* pinions] lend my
        thought;
Grant me, time's Father, world-containing King
A pow'r, of thee in pow'rful lays to sing,
That as thy beauty in earth lives, heaven shines,
So it may dawn or shadow in my lines."

(ll. 1-16.)

At the close he prays:

" What wit cannot conceive, words say of thee,
Here, where, as in a mirror, we but see
Shadows of shadows, atoms of thy might,
Still owly-eyed when staring on thy light,
Grant that, released from this earthly jail,
And freed of clouds which here our knowledge veil,
In heaven's high temples, where thy praises ring,
I may in sweeter notes hear angels sing."

(ll. 329-335.)

" A Prayer for Mankind," however, opens with
the note of humble adoration and a sense of sin.

" Great God, whom we with humble thoughts adore,
    Eternal, infinite, almighty King,

*   *   *   *   *

At whose command clouds dreadful thunders sound!
Ah! spare us worms; weigh not how we, alas

Evil to ourselves, against thy laws rebel;
Wash off those spots which still in mind's clear glass,
Though we be loath to look, we see too well;
Deserv'd revenge O do not, do not take!"

(ll. 1–13.)

It closes similarly:

" Grant, when at last our souls these bodies leave,
Their loathsome shops of sin, and mansions blind,
And doom before thy royal seat receive,
They may a Saviour, not a judge thee find."

(ll. 65–68.)

In Spenser's " Hymne of Heavenly Beautie "
in the first portion of which he sings the ascent
of the mind through ever rising stages of perfection to

" that Highest farre beyond all telling,"

the mingling of these two ways of approach to
God is very apparent. Spenser is first a Platonist and then a Christian. How, he asks, if
God's glory is such that the sun is dimmed by
comparison, can we behold Him?

" The meanes therefore which unto us is lent,
Him to behold, is on his workes to looke,
Which he hath made in beauty excellent,
And in the same, as in a brasen booke,
To reade enregistred in every nooke
His goodnesse, which his beautie doth declare,
For all thats good, is beautifull and faire.

" Thence gathering plumes of perfect speculation,
To impe the wings of thy high flying mynd,
Mount up aloft through heavenly contemplation,
From this darke world, whose damps the soule do blynd,
And like the native brood of Eagles kynd,
On that bright Sunne of glorie fixe thine eyes,
Clear'd from grosse mists of fraile infirmities."

Then comes in the sense of sin, and he approaches God in a different spirit. He continues :

" Humbled with feare and awful reverence,
Before the footestoole of his Maiestie,
Throw thy selfe downe with trembling innocence,
Ne dare looke up with corruptible eye,
On the dred face of that great *Deity*,
For feare, lest if he chaunce to looke on thee,
Thou turne to nought, and quite confounded be.

" But lowly fall before his mercie seate,
Close covered with the Lambes integrity,
From the just wrath of his avengefull threate,
That sits upon the righteous throne on hy."

(ll. 130–152.)

II. NATURE OF THE SOUL

The nature of the soul from the standpoint of Plotinian metaphysics was treated by Henry More in his two poetical treatises, " Pyschathanasia " and "Anti-psychopannychia." In the former he follows the course of the argument

set forth in the seventh book of the fourth
"Ennead" of Plotinus. In the Plotinian defence
two propositions are established ; namely, that
the soul is not body, and that it is not a function of body. By demonstrating these, it followed that the soul is an immaterial thing,
a real being, and consequently eternal. This
is the drift of More's argument in " Psychathanasia." The first and second books are devoted
to the establishment of the definition of the soul
as an incorporeal substance, and the proof of its
incorporeality is deduced from considerations
of its functions.

The soul, More holds, is an incorporeal thing
because it is a self-moving substance present
in all forms of life. Plotinus had taught that
soul was everywhere. " First, then," he says,
" let every soul consider this : how by breath-
ing life into them soul made all animals, the
creatures of earth, sea, air, the divine stars in
heaven ; made the sun, made the great firma-
ment above us, and not only made but ordered
it, so that it swings round in due course. Yet
is this soul a different nature from what it
orders, and moves, and vivifies. It must needs
then be more precious than its creations. For

they are born, and when the soul which min-
isters their life abandons them, they die ; but the
soul ever is because it never abandons itself."
("Enneads," V. i. 2.)   More finds this soul present in the growth of all forms of vegetation, the
sphere spermatic (I. ii. 30), in the life of animals, sensation, and self-directed motion ; and
in the intellectual life of man.   (I. ii. 17–22.)

> " Thus have I trac'd the soul in all its works,
> And severall conditions have displaid,
> And show'd all places where so e'r she lurks,
> Even her own lurkings of her self bewray'd,
> In plants, in beasts, in men, while here she staid."
>
> (I. ii. 23.)

He next demonstrates that this soul is a
self-moving substance.   It is self-moving in
plants, as the quickening power of the sun
on vegetation shows.   Through the heat of
the sun the hidden centre, or soul, is called
into the life of blossoming and growth.

> " Thus called out by friendly sympathie
> Their souls move of themselves on their *Centreitie*."
>
> (I. ii. 31.)

In animals the self-moving soul is manifested
in motion and the life of sensation.

> " Then be the souls of beasts self-moving forms,
> Bearing their bodies as themselves think meet,

Invited or provok'd, so they transform
At first themselves within, then straight in sight
Those motions come, which suddenly do light
Upon the bodies visible, which move
According to the will of th' inward spright."

(I. ii. 36.)

In man the self-motion of the soul is present
in the activity of reason, whether as the pre-
siding power in all of the operations of the
image-making faculty, or as the contemplative
and speculative power.   (I. ii. 41–44.)

After this account of the nature of the soul
as a self-moving substance, More addresses
himself to the task of showing that all life is
immortal.   In a time of despondency a Nymph
once came and declared to him,

" *All life's immortall:* though the outward trunk
May changed be, yet life to nothing never shrunk."

(I. iii. 17.)

According to the theory unfolded by the
Nymph there is an ever present unity in all
things which is the true source of their life.
This is God.   From Him are six descending
degrees of existence, called intellectual, psy-
chical, imaginative, sensitive, plantal, or spermatic.   (I. iii. 23.)   Below all of these is
matter, which is nothing but mere potential-

ity, or the possibility of all created things.
(I. iv. 9.) Though these various degrees of
life are distinct, they are manifestations of the
one pervading unity. (I. iii. 25.) Matter thus
cannot be the prop and stay of life. (I. iii. 26.)

The second proof of the incorporeal nature
of the soul is found in the character of its
functions. After a hasty attack on the doctrine of materialism in the form of a *re-
ductio ad absurdum* (II. ii. 13–25; cf. Plotinus,
IV. vii. 3), More shows, first, that the faculty
within us by which we are aware of the outward world of sense is one and individual, yet
everywhere present in the body. (II. ii. 32.)
This faculty, called "the common sense"
(II. ii. 26), sits as judge over all the data of
sense knowledge (cf. Plotinus, IV. vii. 6); it
decides in case of disagreement between two
senses, and distinguishes clearly between the
objects present to each sense. (II. ii. 28.)
The common sense must be one, else, being
divided, it would breed confusion in consciousness (II. ii. 31); and it must be everywhere
present in the body because it shows no par-
tiality to any sense, but has intelligence of all
equally. (II. ii. 32.)

The rational powers of the soul are a further proof of the soul's incorporeal nature. The first consideration draws attention to the vast scope of man's will and soul. In the virtuous the soul can be so universalized and begotten into the life of God that the will embraces all with a tender love and is ever striving to seek God as the good. (II. iii. 6.) If this is so, More asks whether the soul thus universalized can ever die. (II. iii. 7.) Man's understanding, too, can become so broadened that it can apprehend God's true being, not knowing it, to be sure, in its true essence, but having such a true insight that it can reject all narrow conceptions of His nature and welcome other more comprehensive ideas as closer approximations to the truth. The understanding is in a state that More calls parturient; God under certain conditions can be born within the soul. (II. iii. 9–12.) For the reason, then, of the vastness of the power of will and understanding More holds that the soul cannot be a body. (II. iii. 4.)

The next argument in regard to the rational powers of the soul centres about her power of pure abstraction. (Cf. "Enneads," IV. vii. 8.) In herself the soul divests matter of all time and place relations and views the naked, simple essence of things. (II. iii. 18.) She thus frames within herself an idea, which is indivisible and unextended ; and by this she judges outward objects. (II. iii. 18–20 ; cf. " Enneads," IV. vii. 12.) This property is not a property of body. (II. iii. 26.)

At this point More closes the first division of his argument. By establishing the definition of the soul as a self-moving substance, and by an account of the nature of its functions, he has defended his first proposition, that the soul is an incorporeal thing. He then passes on to the second part of his argument, that the soul is an incorporeal thing because it is independent of the body.

This portion of his defence falls into four main divisions. In the first he explains the nature of the body's dependence upon the soul. Through the power that the soul has by virtue of its lowest centre of life, called the plantal, the soul frames the body in order to exercise through it the functions of life. (III. i. 17.) The more perfect this body is the more awake the soul is. (III. i. 17.) But after the work of framing the body is finished, the soul dismisses it as an old thought and begins its life of contemplation. (III. i. 16.) The main desire is to see God. (III. ii. 11.) Next More shows how the soul can direct her own thoughts within herself without in any way considering the body. Her intellectual part dives within her nature in its quest for self-knowledge and her will affects herself after this knowledge has been gained. All this is accomplished free from any bodily assistance. (III. ii. 25, 26.) The third division shows how the soul is so independent of the body that she can resist its desires. Often the sensual impulse of our nature would lead us to be content with mere satisfaction of our bodily desires ; but the soul desirous of truth and gifted with an insight into God's true nature enables us to resist all such impulses. (III. ii. 38, 39.) The fourth division contrasts the vitality of the soul with that of sense, fancy, and memory. These three faculties are weakened by age and by disease, and also by excessive stimulation ; but the soul never fades, but grows stronger with each contemplative act. (III. ii. 48, 49, 56.)

The attraction which the philosophy of Plotinus had for More's mind lay in its scheme of speculative mysticism. The metaphysical system of Plotinus had taught that The One, which is the truly existing being, is everywhere present and yet nowhere wholly present. ("Enneads," VI. iv.) It had explained also that the only way in which the individual soul could apprehend this truly existing being was by a mystical union with it, in which state the soul did not know in the sense of energizing intellectually, but was one with The One. ("Enneads," VI. ix. 10.) These two ideas lie at the basis of More's theosophic mysticism. Their presence can be felt throughout his "Psychathanasia" as its controlling idea and also in his two less important treatises, "Anti-psychopannychia" and "Anti-monopsychia."

The argument of the "Anti-psychopannychia" and of the "Anti-monopsychia" centres about the doctrine of the mystic union with God. The argument in the "Psychathanasia" is a critique of materialism rather than a positive plea for the existence of the soul after death. It was the purpose of More in his two pendants to his longer poem to treat of the state of the soul after death. That it is not enveloped in eternal night he proves in his

" Anti-psychopannychia." His argument is briefly this. Since God is a unity everywhere present, he is infinite freedom. (II. 2.) Since the soul's activities of will and intellect are free from dependence upon the body, death will be but the ushering of the soul into the life of God's large liberty.

> " Wherefore the soul cut off from lowly sense
>   By harmlesse fate, far greater libertie
>   Must gain : for when it hath departed hence
>   (As all things else) should it not backward hie
>   From whence it came ? but such divinitie
>   Is in our souls that nothing lesse than God
>   Could send them forth (as Plato's schools descrie)
>   Wherefore when they retreat a free abode
>   They'll find, unlesse kept off by *Nemesis* just rod."
>   (II. 14.)

In this life of union the soul will realize the deep fecundity of her own nature ; for in her are innate ideas. To establish this theory of innate ideas into which Plato's theory of reminiscence has been transformed in Plotinus (cf. " Enneads," IV. iii. 25), More educes four considerations. They must exist because (1) like is known only by like (II. 31) ; (2) no object or number of objects can give the soul a universal concept. (II. 36) ; (3) the apprehension of incorporeal things cannot be made by sense, therefore the soul must have the measure of such within her own nature (II. 38, 39) ; and (4) the process of learning shows that it is education, or the drawing out of the mind what was in it potentially (II. 42). Inasmuch, then, as innate ideas exist within the mind, called out by experience in life, how much more will they be evoked in that high union with God !

> " But sith our soul with God himself may meet,
> Inacted by his life, I cannot see
> What scruple then remains that moven might
> Least doubt but that she wakes with open eye,
> When fate her from this body doth untie.
> Wherefore her choisest forms do then arise,
> Rowz'd up by union and large sympathy
> With Gods own spright : she plainly then descries
> Such plentitude of life, as she could nere devise."
>
> (III. 2.)

But this union of the soul with The One may be thought to obliterate self-identity after death and teach only a universal absorption of all souls into The One.   To combat this idea More contends in his " Anti-monopsychia " that by virtue of the " Deiformity " of the soul, by which he means its ability to be joined with God, the soul in death is so

"quickned with near Union
With God, that now wish'd for vitalitie
Is so encreas'd, that infinitely sh' has fun
Herself, her deep'st desire unspeakably hath wonne.

" And deep desire is the deepest act,
    The most profound and centrall energie,
    The very selfnesse of the soul, which backt
    With piercing might, she breaks out, forth doth flie
    From dark contracting death, and doth descrie
    Herself unto herself ; so thus unfold
    That actual life she straightwayes saith, is I."

                                    (Stz. 35, 36.)

In the " Psychathanasia " the Plotinian doctrines of the immanent unity of The One and
of the mystical union of the soul with it are
not so much present as positive arguments in-
corporated in the sequence of thought, but are
felt as controlling ideas in the mind of the
writer. The reason for this lies in the fact
that in the argument of Plotinus (IV. vii)
these two truths of his philosophy are not
specifically elaborated. To More, however, as
indeed to all students of Plotinian metaphysics,
these are the significant ideas of his system.
More thus brings them in at opportune times
throughout his argument in " Psychathanasia."

The conception of the ever present unity of

The One in all things is the fundamental idea
in the first division of his thought. The te-
nacity with which he clings to this doctrine is
remarkable. His argument had brought him
to the point where he had shown that all life
— of plants and animals, as well as of men —
was immortal. What, then, is the state of the
plantal and animal soul after death? (I. ii.
49–53.) More does not answer directly, but
replies that although men cannot know this,
it is not permitted to reason it down.

> " But it's already clear that 'tis not right
>   To reason down the firm subsistencie
>   Of things from ignorance of their propertie."

> (I. ii. 59.)

Consequently when he comes to consider man's
immortality, he says that all the preceding
argument — the general reflection on the "self-
motion and centrall stabilitie" of the soul —
may be dismissed as needless.

> "Onely that vitalitie,
>   That doth extend this great Universall,
>   And move th' inert Materialitie
>   Of great and little worlds, that keep in memorie."

> (II. i. 7.)

It is because of the firm conviction with which
he holds to the conception of the pervading
unity of The One that he expands the idea at
length in the third and fourth cantos of the
first book.

The second idea, that of the mystical union of
the individual soul with The One, is an incen-
tive to More's thought and feelings throughout
the course of his entire argument. From the
fact that the soul can dive as deep as matter,
and rise to the height of a blissful union with
God, he derives the necessary inspiration for
his " mighty task."

" This is the state of th' ever-moving soul,
    Whirling about upon its circling wheel;
    Certes to sight it variously doth roll,
    And as men deem full dangerously doth reel,
    But oft when men fear most, itself doth feel
    In happiest plight conjoin'd with that great Sun
    Of lasting blisse, that doth himself reveal
    More fully then, by that close union,
    Though men, that misse her here, do think her quite
        undone."   (I. ii. 8.)

When in the course of his argument he arrives
at a discussion of the rational power of the
soul, he launches out into a treatment of the
vast scope of man's will and mind which

"should bring forth that live Divinity
Within ourselves, if once God would consent
To shew his specious form and nature eminent:

"For here it lies like colours in the night
Unseen and unregarded, but the sunne
Displayes the beauty and the gladsome plight
Of the adorned earth, while he doth runne
His upper stage. But this high prize is wonne
By curbing sense and the self seeking life
(True Christian mortification)
Thus God will his own self in us revive,
If we to mortifie our straightened selves do strive."

(II. iii. 12, 13.)

Again, when his argument brings him to the
point at which the independence of soul from
body is to be proved, he breaks out with an
exclamation of the bliss of that union of soul
with God, when

"reason shines out bright,
And holy love with mild serenity
Doth hug her harmlesse self in this her purity;"

(III. ii. 28.)

and passes on to a description of The One as
seen in the vision

"Unplac'd, unparted, one close Unity,
Yet omnipresent; all things, yet but one;
Not streak'd with gaudy multiplicity,

Pure light without discolouration,
Stable without circumvolution,
Eternal rest, joy without passing sound."

(III. ii, 36.)

Finally in the last canto of his third book he testifies to the vanity of that knowledge of the reasons for the soul's immortality, even as he had given them (III. ii, 11), and confesses that the only sure stay in the storm of life is a faith in "the first Good."

"But yet, my Muse, still take an higher flight,
Sing of Platonick Faith in the first Good,
That Faith that doth our souls to God unite
So strongly, tightly, that the rapid floud
Of this swift flux of things, nor with foul mud
Can stain, nor strike us off from th' unity,
Wherein we steadfast stand, unshak'd, unmov'd,
Engrafted by a deep vitality
The prop and stay of things is Gods benignity."

(III. iv. 14.)

As in his "Psychozoia" it was noted how the omnipresence of Psyche appealed to More's religious sense of the nearness of God to His children, so in his other treatises, especially his "Psychathanasia," the mystical union of the soul with The One is for More another name for the love of God as known in the soul of the Christian. The Christian religion had taught that God is love, a conception far removed from Platonism, whether of the dialogues or of the "Enneads" of Plotinus. But the tendency to find in Platonism a rational sanction for religious truth was so strong in the theology of the Cambridge school, to which More belonged, that this conception of God as love — which, indeed, is held by the Christian not as an idea but as a fact of his inmost religious experience — was interpreted in the light of the speculative mysticism of Plotinus; and thus the formless One, the ultra-metaphysical principle above all being, became the Christian God of love.

III.   ETERNITY OF THE SOUL AND OF MATTER

In the work of Vaughan and Spenser two distinct phases of another form of Platonic idealism are presented: one in which the poet looks back upon eternity as a fact of the soul's past experience, and the other in which he directs a forward glance to the future when the soul shall find its eternal rest.

In the expression of his sense of eternity, Vaughan recurs to the doctrine of the pre-

existence of the soul as it is expounded in Plato.
In Vaughan this idea is felt as an influence
either affording the substance of his thought or
determining the nature of his imagery. The
idea which Vaughan carries over into his
own poetry is found in Plato's account in the
" Phædrus " of the preëxistence of the soul in
a world of pure ideas before its descent into the
body. " There was a time," says Plato, " when
with the rest of the happy band they [*i.e.* the
human souls] saw beauty shining in brightness : we philosophers following in the train of
Zeus, others in company with other gods ; and
then we beheld the beatific vision and were
initiated into a mystery which may be truly
called most blessed, celebrated by us in our
state of innocence, before we had any experience of evils to come, when we were admitted
to the sight of apparitions innocent and simple
and calm and happy, which we held shining in
pure light, pure ourselves and not yet enshrined
in that living tomb which we carry about, now
that we are imprisoned in the body, like an
oyster in his shell." (" Phædrus," 250.)

This idea occurs in two forms in Vaughan.
In " The Retreat " the reminiscence of a past

is described as a fact of Vaughan's religious
experience. He longs to travel back to the
time when, in his purity, he was nearer to God
than he is now in his sinful state.

> " Happy those early days, when I
> Shin'd in my angel-infancy !
> Before I understood this place
> Appointed for my second race,
> Or taught my soul to fancy ought
> But a white, celestial thought ;
> When yet I had not walk'd above
> A mile or two from my first love,
> And looking back — at that short space —
> Could see a glimpse of His bright face ;
> When on some gilded cloud, or flow'r,
> My gazing soul would dwell an hour,
> And in those weaker glories spy
> Some shadows of eternity ;
> Before I taught my tongue to wound
> My conscience with a sinful sound,
> Or had the black art to dispence
> A sev'ral sin to ev'ry sense,
> But felt through all this fleshly dress
> Bright shoots of everlastingness.
> O how I long to travel back,
> And tread again that ancient track !
> That I might once more reach that plain,
> Where first I left my glorious train :
> From whence th' enlighten'd spirit sees
> That shady City of palm-trees.
> But ah ! my soul with too much stay
> Is drunk, and staggers in the way !

Some men a forward motion love,
But I by backward steps would move;
And when this dust falls to the urn,
In that state I came, return."

The second form of this idea appears in
Vaughan's poem called " Corruption." Man
is represented as enjoying the happiness of
innocence in the garden of Eden, where he
was in close touch with the beauties of heaven.
Here he had a glimpse of his heavenly birth;
but when, by reason of sin, he was forced to
leave that place, he found earth and heaven no
longer friendly.

" Sure, it was so. Man in those early days
    Was not all stone and earth;
He shin'd a little, and by those weak rays
    Had some glimpse of his birth.
He saw heaven o'er his head, and knew from whence
    He came, condemnèd, hither;
And, as first love draws strongest, so from hence
    His mind sure progress'd thither.
Things here were strange unto him; sweat and till;
    All was a thorn or weed.
            *   *   *   *   *
This made him long for home, as loth to stay
    With murmurers and foes;
He sigh'd for Eden, and would often say
    ' Ah! what bright days were those!'
Nor was heav'n cold unto him : for each day
    The valley or the mountain

Afforded visits, and still Paradise lay
In some green shade or fountain.
Angels lay leiger here: each bush, and cell,
Each oak, and highway knew them;
Walk but the fields, or sit down at some well,
And he was sure to view them."

In this poem, although there is no such parallelism with the account of a preëxistent state as it is given in Plato, the fundamental idea is the same as that of " The Retreat." Vaughan describes man's life in Eden as one of closer intimacy with his celestial home than his lot on earth affords him, just as he had described the experience of his own "angel-infancy" and its contrast to his earthly life. In both poems is present the conviction that the human soul once lived in a state of pure innocence; and in both is heard the note of regret at the loss of this through sin.

In Vaughan's poem, " The World," the influence of Plato's account of the preëxistent life of the soul is felt only in affording the character of the imagery which Vaughan has used to express his idea. In the "Phædrus" Plato describes the progress of the soul in its sight of the eternal ideas in the heaven of heavens. Each soul, represented as a charioteer guiding a pair of winged horses, is carried about by the revolution of the spheres, and during the progress it beholds the ideas. The souls of the gods have no difficulty in seeing these realities; "but of the other souls," says Plato, "that which follows God best and is likest to him lifts the head of the charioteer into the outer world, and is carried round in the revolution, troubled indeed by the steeds, and with difficulty beholding true being; while another only rises and falls, and sees, and again fails to see by reason of the unruliness of the steeds. The rest of the souls are also longing after the upper world, and they all follow, but not being strong enough they are carried round below the surface, plunging, treading on one another, each striving to be first; and there is confusion and perspiration and the extremity of effort; and many of them are lamed, or have their wings broken, through the ill-driving of the charioteers." ("Phædrus," 248.)

In this account of the revolution of the soul about the eternal realities of true being, Vaughan found the suggestion for his poem, "The World." Instead of the revolution of the soul about true being, he describes the revolution of time about eternity. The figure of the charioteer is absent, too, but it is by the use of the "wing" that those who make the revolution about eternity mount up into the circle, just as in Plato. Time in the poem also is represented as being "driven about by the spheres." Such coincidences of imagery show that Vaughan found in Plato's fanciful account of the soul's preëxistent life in heaven the medium through which he expressed his view of the relation of the life of the present day world to that of eternity. At first he pictures the revolution of the world about the great ring of light which he calls eternity:

"I saw Eternity the other night,
  Like a great ring of pure and endless light,
    All calm, as it was bright;
  And round beneath it, Time in hours, days, years,
    Driv'n by the spheres
  Like a vast shadow mov'd: in which the world
  And all her train were hurl'd."

He then describes the lover busied in his trifles, — his lute, his fancies, and his delights. Next moves the statesman, pursued by the shouts of multitudes. The next to follow are the miser and the epicure.

" The doting lover in his quaintest strain
     Did there complain;
Near him, his lute, his fancy, and his flights,
     Wit's sour delights;
With gloves, and knots, the silly snares of pleasure
     Yet his dear treasure,
All scatter'd lay, while he his eyes did pour
     Upon a flow'r.

" The darksome statesman, hung with weights and woe,
Like a thick midnight fog, mov'd there so slow,
     He did nor stay, nor go;
Condemning thoughts — like sad eclipses — scowl
     Upon his soul,
And clouds of crying witnesses without
     Pursued him with one shout.

       *   *   *   *   *

" The fearful miser on a heap of rust
Sate pining all his life there, did scarce trust
     His own hands with the dust,
Yet would not place one piece above, but lives
     In fear of thieves.
Thousands there were as frantic as himself,
     And hugg'd each one his pelf;
The downright epicure plac'd heav'n in sense,
     And scorn'd pretence;
While others, slipp'd into a wide excess,
     Said little less;
The weaker sort slight, trivial wares enslave,
     Who think them brave;
And poor, despisèd Truth sate counting by
     Their victory."

At this point Vaughan ends his catalogue of
human types and comments upon the unwill-
ingness of the many to soar up into the ring
by the aid of the wing.

> " Yet some, who all this while did weep and sing,
>   And sing, and weep, soar'd up into the ring;
>   But most would use no wing.
>   O fools — said I — thus to prefer dark night
>   Before true light !
>   To live in grots and caves, and hate the day
>   Because it shows the way ;
>   The way, which from this dead and dark abode
>   Leads up to God."

Spenser finds his suggestion of the eternal in
life, not in a consciousness of a past existence,
but in a conception of the world of matter built
up in accordance with the Platonic doctrine
of stability of the substance amid the flux of
changing forms.   This conception of the world
is explained by him in his description of the
" Garden of Adonis " in the " Faerie Queene "
and in his " Two Cantos of Mutabilitie."

The conception of matter which Spenser
teaches is the doctrine of Plotinus expressed in
accordance with the account of flux and stability of natural phenomena explained by Plato

in the "Timæus." According to Plotinus
matter is an indestructible "subject" of forms
which endures through all the various changes
which it is constantly undergoing, and this
unchanging something is never destroyed.
("Enneads," II. iv. 6.) In the "Timæus" Plato
had outlined a theory of flux with which this
doctrine of the indestructibility of matter could
be easily harmonized. In his discussion of the
world of natural phenomena he distinguishes
three natures, as he calls them, and likens them
to a father, a child, and a mother. "For the
present," he says in the "Timæus" (50), "we
have only to conceive of three natures: first,
that which is in process of generation ; secondly,
that in which the generation takes place ; and
thirdly, that of which the thing generated is a
resemblance. And we may liken the receiving
principle to a mother, and the source or spring
to a father, and the intermediate nature to
a child." According to this piece of poetic
imagery he describes the various manifestations
of matter in the outward world. The elements
are constantly changing in and out of one
another and have in them nothing permanent.
They cannot be called "this" or "that," but

only "such." Only the receiving principle, the universal nature, "that must be always called the same ; for while receiving all things, she never departs at all from her own nature, and never in any way or at any time assumes a form like that of any of the things which enter into her ; she is the natural recipient of all impressions, and is stirred and informed by them, and appears different from time to time by reason of them." ("Timæus," 50.)

The explanation of the myriad changes of matter of the outward world of sense after the manner of this account by Plato is found in Spenser's description of the "Garden of Adonis." The term "garden of Adonis" is found in Plato's "Phædrus" (276), where is meant an earthen vessel in which plants are nourished to quick growth only to decay as rapidly. On this term Spenser's imagination built its superstructure of fancy by which the garden of Adonis became symbolic of the world of natural phenomena described after the manner of Plato in the "Timæus" and Plotinus in the "Enneads." The garden is described at first as a seminary of all living things, conceived first as flowers :

" In that same Gardin all the goodly flowres,
　Wherewith dame Nature doth her beautifie,
　And decks the girlonds of her paramoures,
　Are fetcht : there is the first seminarie
　Of all things, that are borne to live and die,
　According to their kindes.   Long worke it were,
　Here to account the endlesse progenie
　Of all the weedes, that bud and blossome there ;
　But so much as doth need, must needs be counted here."

(III. vi. 30.)

Spenser's imagination now changes, and he conceives of the objects in this garden as naked babes, in accordance with the suggestion of the intermediate nature which Plato conceived as a child.   Genius as the porter of the place is thus described :

" He letteth in, he letteth out to wend,
　All that to come into the world desire ;
　A thousand thousand naked babes attend
　About him day and night, which doe require,
　That he with fleshly weedes would them attire :
　Such as him list, such as eternal fate
　Ordained hath, he clothes with sinfull mire,
　And sendeth forth to live in mortall state,
　Till they againe returne backe by the hinder gate."

(III. vi. 32.)

Again there is a change, and the objects issuing from this garden are forms which borrow their substance from the matter of chaos.

" Infinite shapes of creatures there are bred,
  And uncouth formes, which none yet ever knew,
  And every sort is in a sundry bed
  Set by it selfe, and ranckt in comely rew
  Some fit for reasonable soules t' indew,
  Some made for beasts, some made for birds to weare,
  And all the fruitfull spawne of fishes hew
  In endlesse rancks along enraunged were,
  That seem'd the *Ocean* could not containe them there."

                                        (III. vi. 35.)

When these forms are sent forth from the
garden they take for their substance the matter
found in chaos which is ever eternal.

" Daily they grow, and daily forth are sent
  Into the world, it to replenish more;
  Yet is the stocke not lessened, nor spent,
  But still remaines in everlasting store,
  As it at first created was of yore.
  For in the wide wombe of the world there lyes,
  In hateful darkenesse and in deepe horrore,
  An huge eternall *Chaos*, which supplyes
  The substances of natures fruitfull progenyes.

" All things from thence doe their first being fetch,
  And borrow matters whereof they are made,
  Which when as forme and feature it doth ketch,
  Becomes a bodie, and doth then invade
  The state of life, out of the griesly shade.
  That substance is eterne, and bideth so,
  Ne when the life decayes, and forme does fade,

Doth it consume, and into nothing go,
But chaunged is, and often altred to and fro."

                              (III. vi. 36–37.)

Spenser now stops the play of fancy and
becomes the philosopher, explaining the doctrine of matter as taught by Plotinus. The
substance of things is eternal and abides in
potency of further change.

" The substance is not changed, nor altered,
    But th' only forme and outward fashion;
    For every substance is conditioned
    To change her hew, and sundry formes to don,
    Meet for her temper and complexion:
    For formes are variable and decay,
    By course of kind, and by occasion;
    And that faire flower of beautie fades away,
    As doth the lilly fresh before the sunny ray."

                              (II. vi. 38.)

Finally, Spenser closes his account of the
garden with a mingling of fancy and philosophy. He adopts the suggestion of Plato that
the source of the many changes in natural
phenomena is a father, and blends the conception with the myth of Venus and Adonis. In
the garden Venus is represented as enjoying
the pleasure of the presence of Adonis per-
petually, for he is described as the father of

the various forms who abides eternal in all change.

" There wont faire *Venus* often to enjoy
   Her deare *Adonis* joyous company,
   And reape sweet pleasure of the wanton boy;
   There yet, some say, in secret he does ly,
   Lapped in flowers and pretious spycery,
   By her hid from the world, and from the skill
   Of *Stygian* Gods, which doe her love envy;
   But she her selfe, when ever that she will,
   Possesseth him, and of his sweetnesse takes her fill.

" And sooth it seemes they say : for he may not
   For ever die, and ever buried bee
   In balefull night, where all things are forgot;
   All be he subject to mortalitie,
   Yet is eterne in mutabilitie,
   And by succession made perpetuall,
   Transformed oft, and chaunged diverslie :
   For him the Father of all formes they call;
   Therefore needs mote he live, that living gives to all."
                                    (III. vi. 46, 47.)

The attraction which this doctrine of the indestructibility of matter had for Spenser lay in the comforting assurance which it brought him of an eternity when things should be at rest.   Throughout Spenser is heard a note of world weariness.

" Nothing is sure, that growes on earthly ground."

These words placed in the mouth of Arthur
(I. ix. 11) are essentially characteristic of
Spenser's outlook on the things of this world:
they are his *lacrimæ rerum*. The "Cantos of
Mutabilitie" is the best instance in point.
These two cantos celebrate the overthrow of
Mutability by Nature. To the claim of preëmi-
nence among the gods which Mutability lays
before Nature, and which she bases upon the
fact that everything in the wide universe is subject to constant change, Dame Nature replies that
though they be subject to change, they change
only their outward state, each change working
their perfection ; and she further remarks that
the time will come when there shall be no more
change. At the end of Mutability's plea Dame
Nature thus answers the charge :

" I well consider all that ye have sayd,
  And find that all things stedfastnes doe hate
  And changed be: yet being rightly wayd
  They are not changed from their first estate ;
  But by their change their being doe dilate :
  And turning to themselves at length againe,
  Doe worke their owne perfection so by fate :
  Then over them Change doth not rule and raigne ;
  But they raigne over change, and doe their states main-
     taine.

" Cease therefore daughter further to aspire,
  And thee content thus to be rul'd by me :
  For thy decay thou seekst by thy desire;
  But time shall come that all shall changed bee,
  And from thenceforth, none no more change shall see."

(VII. vii. 58, 59.)

On this decision of Nature Spenser bases his
assurance of a time when the soul shall have
its final rest. With a prayer to the great God
of Sabaoth that he may see the time when all
things shall rest in Him, Spenser closes his
work on his great unfinished poem — the
" Faerie Queene."

" Then gin I thinke on that which Nature sayd,
  Of that same time when no more *Change* shall be,
  But stedfast rest of all things firmely stayd
  Upon the pillours of Eternity,
  That is contrayr to *Mutabilitie :*
  For, all that moveth, doth in *Change* delight:
  But thence-forth all shall rest eternally.
  With Him that is the God of Sabbaoth hight:
  O Thou great Sabbaoth God, graunt me that Sabaoths
      sight."

(VII. viii. 2.)

In the theory of the preëxistence of the soul
and in the conception of the indestructibility of
matter Vaughan and Spenser were able to find
teachings which were akin to the most intimate

experiences of their lives. Although the phase
of Platonic idealism which taught in these two
distinct ways the eternity of human life and of
the world about us did not have so vital an influence upon English poetry as did the opening
of a world of moral beauty, its presence is never-
theless indicative of the strong hold which Platonism had upon some of the finest poetic minds
of the sixteenth and seventeenth centuries in
England. Even when these poets were writing
from the fulness of their own personal experience, it was in the moulds of Platonic philosophy that their thought was cast.

The elements of Platonism, then, that enter
into the English poetry of the sixteenth and
seventeenth centuries, have their source in the
dialogues of Plato and the "Enneads" of Plotinus. The body of this teaching—its æsthetics,
its metaphysics, and its ethics — was seen by the
poets in its relation to Christian doctrine and
to the passion of romantic love. The more
permanent results for good are found in the
fusion of Platonism with the ideals of Christian
living and with its longing for perfection. If
one passage in Plato may adequately sum up
the teaching of Platonism most influential in

English poetry, it is the passage in " Phædrus "
in which the beauty of wisdom is taught
("Phædrus," 250).

But beauty in its stricter import is a thing
known to the sense, and is carried over into the
moral world only to indicate the value of moral
ideas. Plato recognized this; and in this connection it is significant that in the part of
"Phædrus," where he speaks of the loveliness
of wisdom, he is aware of the power of pure
beauty. "But of beauty," he says, "I repeat
again that we saw her there [in the ideal world]
shining in company with the celestial forms;
and coming to earth we find her here too, shining in clearness through the clearest aperture of
sense. For sight is the most piercing of our
bodily senses; though not by that is wisdom
seen; her loveliness would have been transporting if there had been a visible image of her,
and the other ideas, if they had visible counter-
parts, would be equally lovely. But this is the
privilege of beauty, that being the loveliest she
is also the most palpable to sight " (250).

Spenser was the poet who caught the spirit
of this teaching. Pastorella's beauty is presented not as Una's, the beauty of wisdom, nor

as Britomart's, the beauty of the inward purity
of womanhood; but it is a beauty of pure form.

> " And soothly sure she was full fayre of face,
>   And perfectly well shapt in every lim,
>   Which she did more augment with modest grace,
>   And comely carriage of her count'nance trim,
>   That all the rest like lesser lamps did dim."
>
> (VI. ix. 9.)

And yet as she stands on the little hillock she
is encompassed with a cloud of glory.

> " Upon a litle hillocke she was placed
>   Higher then all the rest, and round about
>   Environ'd with a girland, goodly graced,
>   Of lovely lasses, and them all without
>   The lustie shepheard swaynes sate in a rout;
>   The which did pype and sing her prayses dew,
>   And oft rejoyce, and oft for wonder shout,
>   As if some miracle of heavenly hew
>   Were downe to them descended in that earthly vew."
>
> (VI. ix. 8.)

They saw in the object before their eyes the
idea of beauty in earthly form. The miracle
is no more and no less than this; it is " the
privilege of beauty, that being the loveliest she
is also the most palpable to sight."

BIBLIOGRAPHY

ARISTOTLE. " The Nicomachean Ethics of Aristotle,"
translated into English by Robert Williams.
London, 1869.

AYRES, PHILIP. " Lyric Poems." London, 1687.

AYTOUN, ROBERT. " Poems," edited by Charles Rogers.
London, 1871.

BIGG, C. " Neo-platonism." London, 1895.

BOYLE, ROBERT. "A Treatise of Seraphic Love." Edinburgh, 1825.

BROME, ALEXANDER. " Songs and Other Poems." Second edition. 1664.

CAMPION, THOMAS. " Works," edited by A. H. Bullen.
London, 1889.

CAREW, THOMAS. " Poems," edited by Arthur Vincent.
London and New York, 1899.

CARTWRIGHT, WILLIAM. " Comedies, Tragi-comedies
with Other Poems." London, 1651.

CHARLETON, WALTER. " The Ephesian and Cimmerian
Matrons." London, 1668.

CLEVELAND, JOHN. " Works." London, 1687.

COWLEY, ABRAHAM. " Works." 2 vols. Eleventh edition. London, 1710.

CRAIG, ALEXANDER. " Poetical Works," printed for
the Hunterian Club, 1873.

CRASHAW, RICHARD. "Complete Works," edited by A.
B. Grosart. 2 vols. 1873.

DANIEL, GEORGE. "Poems," edited by A. B. Grosart. 4 vols. 1878.

DANIEL, SAMUEL. "Complete Works in Verse and Prose," edited by A. B. Grosart. 4 vols. 1885.

D'AVENANT, WILLIAM. "Dramatic Works," edited by James Maidment and W. H. Logan. 5 vols. Edinburgh and London, 1872–1874.

DE VERE, AUBREY THOMAS. "Characteristics of Spenser's Poetry" and "Spenser as a Philosophic Poet," in "Essays, chiefly on Poetry." 2 vols. London, 1887.

DODGE, R. E. NEIL. "Spenser's Imitations from Ariosto," in "Publications of Modern Language Association of America," 1897.

DONNE, JOHN. "Works," edited by Henry Alford. 6 vols. London, 1839.
"Poems," edited by E. K. Chambers, with an introduction by George Saintsbury. 2 vols. London and New York, 1896.

DOWDEN, EDWARD. "Puritan and Anglican Studies in Literature." New York, 1901.

DRAYTON, MICHAEL. "Poems." London, 1613.
"Poemes, Lyrick and Pastorall," printed for the Spenser Society. 1891.

DRUMMOND, WILLIAM. "Poems," edited by William C. Ward. 2 vols. London and New York, 1894.
"Ben Jonson's Conversations with William Drummond." Shakespeare Society Publications, vol. 8.

DRYDEN, JOHN. "Works," edited by Sir Walter Scott, revised by George Saintsbury. 18 vols. Edinburgh, 1887.

EINSTEIN, LEWIS. "Italian Renaissance in England." New York, 1902.

FERRI, LUIGI. "Platonismo di Ficino," in "La Filoso-
fia delle Scuole Italiane," vol. 29, pp. 269–294.

FICINUS, MARSILIUS. "Commentarium in Convivium,"
in "Omnia Divini Platonis Opera." Basileae, 1551.

FLETCHER, GILES. "Complete Poems," edited by A. B.
Grosart. London, 1876.

FLETCHER, J. B. "Précieuses at the Court of Charles I,"
in the "Journal of Comparative Literature," vol. 1,
pp. 120–153.

FLETCHER, PHINEAS. "Poems," edited by A. B. Grosart.
4 vols. 1869.

GREVILLE, FULKE. "Works," edited by A. B. Grosart.
4 vols. 1870.

HABINGTON, WILLIAM. "Castara," edited by Charles
A. Elton. Bristol, 1812.

HERBERT, EDWARD, Lord Herbert of Cherbury. "Poems,"
edited by John Churton Collins. London, 1881.

HERBERT, GEORGE. "Poetical Works," edited by A. B.
Grosart. London, 1876.

HEYWOOD, THOMAS. "Love's Mistress or the Queen's
Masque," edited by Edmund Goldsmid. Edinburgh, 1886.

HOWELL, JAMES. "Familiar Letters," edited by Joseph
Jacobs. 2 vols. 1892.
"Lustra Ludovicii." London, 1648.

INGE, WILLIAM RALPH. "Christian Mysticism." New
York, 1899.

JONSON, BEN. "Works," with notes by William Gif-
ford, edited by Lt. Col. Francis Cunningham.
3 vols. London, 1871.

LINCHE, RICHARD. "Diella," edited by A. B. Grosart, in
"Occasional Issues of Unique or very Rare Books,"
vol. 4. 1877.

LOVELACE, RICHARD. "Lucasta," edited by W. Carew Hazlitt. London, 1864.

LOWELL, JAMES RUSSELL. "Spenser," in "Works," vol. 4. Riverside edition, 1898.

MASSON, DAVID. "Life of John Milton." 6 vols. Cambridge, 1859–1880.

MILTON, JOHN. "Poetical Works," edited by David Masson. 3 vols. London, 1874.
"Prose Works," edited by Charles Symmons. 7 vols. London, 1806.

MORE, HENRY. "Psychodia Platonica, or a Platonicall Song of the Soul consisting of . . . Psychozoia, Psychathanasia, Anti-psychopannychia, Anti-monopsychia." Cambridge, 1642.

NORRIS, JOHN. "A Collection of Miscellanies." London, 1706.

PARKER, SAMUEL. "A Free and Impartial Censure of the Platonick Philosophie." Second edition. Oxford, 1667.

PLATO. "Dialogues of Plato," translated into English by B. Jowett. 5 vols. New York, 1892.

PLOTINUS. "Opera Omnia . . . cum Marsilii Ficini Commentariis," edited by Frederick Creuzer. 3 vols. Oxford, 1835.
"On Suicide," "Two Books on Truly Existing Being," "Extracts from Treatise on the Manner in which the Multitude of Ideas subsist, and concerning the Good." Translations by Thomas Taylor. London, 1834.

RANDOLPH, THOMAS. "Poetical and Dramatic Works," edited by W. Carew Hazlitt. 2 vols. London, 1875.

SEDLEY, CHARLES. "Works." 2 vols. London, 1722.

SHAKESPEARE, WILLIAM. "Poems," edited by George
    Wyndham. London, 1898.
SIDNEY, PHILIP. "Astrophel and Stella," edited by
    Ewald Flügel. Halle, 1889.
    "The Countess of Pembroke's Arcadia," edited
    by H. Oskar Sommer. London, 1891.
SPENSER, EDMUND. "Complete Works," edited by A. B.
    Grosart. 10 vols. 1882–1884.
    "Faerie Queene." Book I, edited by H. M.
    Percival. London, 1894.
    "Faerie Queene." Book II, edited by G. W.
    Kitchin. London, 1868.
STANLEY, THOMAS. "Poems." London, 1814.
SUCKLING, JOHN. "Poems, Plays, and Other Remains,"
    edited by W. Carew Hazlitt. 2 vols. London,
    1892.
TULLOCH, JOHN. "Rational Theology and Christian
    Philosophy in England in the Seventeenth Cen-
    tury." Second edition. 2 vols. Edinburgh, 1874.
VAUGHAN, HENRY. "Poems," edited by E. K. Cham-
    bers, with an introduction by H. C. Beeching.
    2 vols. London and New York, 1896.
WALTON, IZAAK. "Complete Angler and the Lives of
    Donne, Wotton, Hooker, Herbert, and Sanderson."
    London, 1901.
WARD, HENRY. "Life of Henry More." London, 1710.
WHITTAKER, THOMAS. "The Neo-Platonists: a Study
    in the History of Hellenism." Cambridge, 1901.

INDEX

229

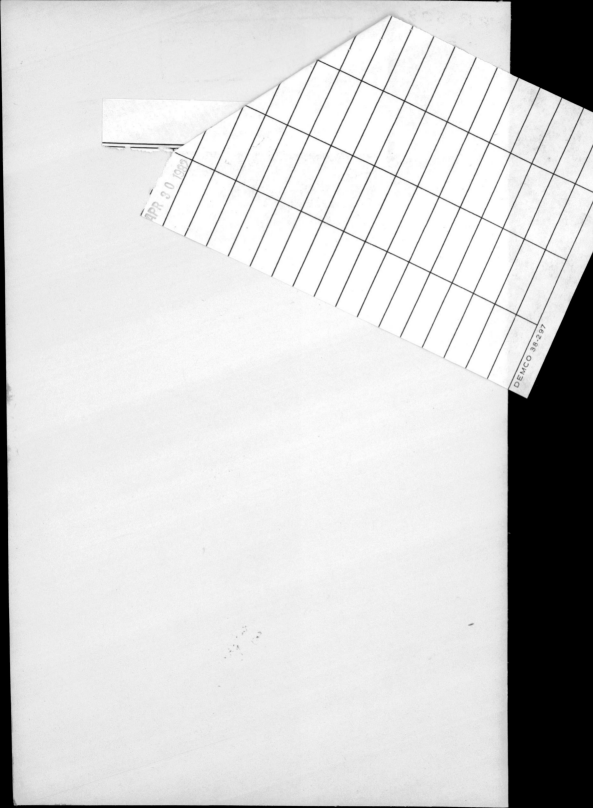